HOMILY OUTLINES FOR LENT

ACKNOWLEDGMENTS

The Scripture Texts from *The New American Bible* © 1970 by The Confraternity of Christian Doctrine are used herein by license of said copyright owner. All rights reserved.

Imprimi Potest: Rev. Charles Terrence Quinn, O.P.
                     Provincial
                     January 16, 1976

Nihil Obstat: Rev. John J. Sullivan, O.P.
                     Censor Deputatus
                     January 19, 1977

Imprimatur: William Cardinal Baum
                     Archbishop of Washington
                     January 19, 1977

Library of Congress Catalog Number: LC77-70337
ISBN: 0-918344-01-8

HOMILY OUTLINES FOR LENT

SUNDAYS CYCLE C AND WEEKDAYS

DANIEL B. CROWLEY, O.P.

HARRY COSTELLO PUBLISHING COMPANY, INC.
Post Office Box 9, Northport, New York 11768

DEDICATED

TO

A FRIEND

TABLE OF CONTENTS

FOREWORD

Encouraged by the reception given my previous volume, I am pleased to offer this work to my brother priests, with the hope that it will assist them in the preparation of their homilies. Each Sunday outline develops a thought contained in one of the readings for the Sundays of Lent, while each weekday outline is based on the Responsorial Psalm for the day.

Following the format of the previous work, every outline of the present volume has two major divisions which are in turn subdivided. The user of this book is therefore free to select the material presented and to adapt it to the needs of his particular congregation. It is obvious that the parish priest, the prison chaplain, the person involved in the campus ministry, and the chaplain at a cloistered monastery will use these outlines in different ways.

A priest may wish to utilize the whole outline, or he may prefer to select certain parts of an outline for his homily. Perhaps these outlines will also serve to stimulate prayerful reflection during Lent, or they may be developed as themes for Days of Recollection or Spiritual Renewal Days.

Offering these outlines to my fellow priests, I pray that together we may fulfill the words God spoke to Isaiah: "Comfort, give comfort to my people" (Isa. 40:1).

INTRODUCTION

The Fathers of the Second Vatican Council remind us that all men are called to holiness. Kindly they explain for us in the document "Constitution on the Sacred Liturgy" that the Liturgy and Sacred Scripture are the chief fonts of Spirituality.

This present volume, like its predecessor, is presented as a help to the priest who in the liturgical celebration of the Paschal Mystery must explain the Word of God to the People of God. It is my wish that many souls who sincerely "seek the face of the God of Abraham, the God is Isaac, and the God of Jacob" may find in this work ideas which they can prayerfully develop in their conversations with God.

No attempt has been made to be different or to startle my readers. This work does not claim to be an original creation; many sources have been used. After twenty-five years in the priesthood I offer this work as the fruit of my extensive reading and my conversations with the numerous priests, sisters, and members of the laity who have contributed to my long and happy years as a Retreat Master.

Obviously, other topics than those I have selected could be used in a daily homily, for the Sacred Text supplies many thoughts for prayer and preaching. My job is to share with you some of my thoughts, and I pray that we may come to a greater realization of the truth that "it is of this fulness that we have all received grace for grace."

ACKNOWLEDGMENTS

Through the years many people have encouraged me to prepare a work of this nature. Time and space limit me in the naming of each individual, but I must mention my Dominican brothers, P. F. Mulhern, J. T. Carrigon, J. J. Sullivan, and R. Smith, who encouraged me and supported me in this effort. Through the years my religious superiors have been most kind, allowing me both time and opportunity to preach and to write. To all who have encouraged me I owe a debt of gratitude.

I must thank Ruth Hannon for her help and kind suggestions in preparing this manuscript for publication. A true friend, Harry Costello, has been kind and generous in his willingness to publish this book. I thank him.

Typing these pages has not been an easy task. I acknowledge my indebtedness to Patty Martini, Betty Antibus and Gillian Stormont, Margaret Madden and Stelle Moore, for the time and effort they gave to typing this manuscript.

ASH WEDNESDAY

Introduction: The Church invites us to consider our dignity during this Lenten season. Signing us with the cross in ashes, the Church reminds us of our dignity. The Church also teaches us how to live the dignified life of a Christian. We are to live as "ambassadors for Christ, God as it were appealing through us" (II Cor. 5:20).

I Our dignity is that of an "ambassador for Christ" (II Cor. 5:20).
  A. Dignity is attached to the office of ambassador.
    1. A nation confers an honor on an individual whom it selects to be its ambassador in a foreign country.
      a. An ambassador is the representative of his country in the land to which he is accredited.
      b. An ambassador must be officially approved by his own government and officially accepted by the host government.
    2. The function of an ambassador is to protect and advance the interests of his country in another land.
      a. To fulfill his role in a foreign land, an ambassador acts in the name of his country's leader.
      b. Keeping in mind the welfare of his country, an ambassador must search for ways to unite in peace and harmony his own country with the country to which he is accredited.
  B. "We are ambassadors for Christ" (II Cor. 5:20).
    1. A great dignity was conferred on us when we were accredited as ambassadors for Christ.
      a. In baptism we were selected by Christ to be his ambassadors.
      b. In baptism we were conformed to Christ the priest.
        1.) For this reason we act in the name of Christ, praying in his name as we attend Mass.
        2.) For this reason we can perform our acts of charity in the name of Christ.
    2. The liturgy of Ash Wednesday reminds us of our dignity as Christ's ambassadors.
      a. We are signed with ashes to emphasize this role.
        1.) The ashes recall to us that during our life on earth we are dwelling in a foreign land.
        2.) Our true country is the kingdom of God.

b. The cross also reminds us of our role as ambassadors for
Christ.
1.)To carry the cross of Christ daily dignifies us.
2.) We are dignified when we live the mystery of the
redemption by dying to ourselves that we may live for
God.

II As ambassadors representing Christ, we are to advance the kingdom of God on earth.
  A. We represent Christ before the world.
    1. It is the teaching of the Fathers of the Second Vatican
    Council that we are to remind men of God.
      a. When people meet an ambassador from another country
      they think of that country and its leader.
      b. We, as God's ambassadors, are to remind men of his pres-
      ence, his goodness, and his mercy.
    2. The works of fasting, prayer, and charity are the fulfillment
    of our role as ambassadors for Christ.
      a. These works are not to be undertaken only in Lent, but
      they are given special emphasis in this season.
      b. These works are a lifetime expression of our ambassador-
      ship.
        1.) Fasting is a sign of God's mercy; by fasting we ask
        God's forgiveness of our sins and remind other men
        that God does forgive repentant sinners.
        2.) Prayer calls to mind the presence of God, for it is a con-
        versation with God who is present to all men.
        3.) Charity is a sign to men of God's goodness; in charity
        we share with others the good things of life we have
        received from God.
  B. As ambassadors for Christ we promote the kingdom of God on
  earth.
    1. St. Paul describes this aspect of our ambassadorial role as
    "God as it were appealing through us" (II Cor. 5:20).
      a. God uses us to sanctify the world; the Second Vatican
      Council pointed out that the world is to be sanctified in
      its secular aspects.
        1.) Our role as ambassadors for Christ is not confined to
        those moments in which we attend Mass or say our
        daily prayers, nor is it bound by the walls of a church.
        2.) We are the means by which the grace of God is

      inserted into every aspect of human life and activity.
  b. As ambassadors for Christ we are to plead his cause.
    1.) We are to exert an influence in the political, economic,
      and social spheres of human activity.
    2.) We are to keep in mind the supernatural destiny of ev-
      ery human being and do all we can to make it possible
      for our fellowmen to pray and to practice virtue.
 2. Lenten practices advance the kingdom of God on earth.
  a. Fasting reminds us that we were not made for sensual
    gratification, but for the glory of the resurrection.
  b. Prayer anticipates on earth the great work of heaven: the
    praise and glorification of God.
  c. Charity prepares souls for the perfect, unending love of
    the kingdom of God.

Conclusion: The sign of the cross, traced in ashes on our foreheads, is not a badge of shame. It is a sign of dignity. It is the renewal of our accreditation as ambassadors for Christ. "We are ambassadors for Christ, God as it were appealing through us" (II Cor. 5:20).

THURSDAY AFTER ASH WEDNESDAY

Introduction: Very early in Lent the Church indicates the choices offered us every day of our lives. Basically the liturgy points out that we have a choice between happiness and misery, between good and evil. That we may make a responsible choice, the first psalm used in today's liturgy contrasts the life of a happy person with the life of one who has not experienced true joy. This psalm makes it clear that a good person is a happy one, while the wicked individual lives a life of misery.

I In human nature there is an inclination to seek happiness.
  A. All our actions are motivated by a desire to be happy.
    1. If we are asked why we perform a particular action, the an-
      swer will surely be, "I want to be happy."
    2. We may not always be consciously aware of the reason for
      our actions.
      a. At least unconsciously we know that what we are doing or
        are about to do will contribute to our happiness.
      b. It is against human nature to want to be miserable.

B. The problem of where and how to find happiness is a vexing one.

1. The great friends of humanity have addressed themselves to this question.

   a. With great compassion for suffering humanity they wanted to eliminate the causes of pain.

   b. The programs for social reform initiated by compassionate leaders are meant to be contributions to human happiness.

      1.) Experience has taught that these plans do contribute to a degree of human happiness by offering relief from suffering.

      2.) On the other hand, such plans do not completely satisfy the craving of the human heart for happiness.

2. In our individual lives we must answer the question of where and how happiness is to be found.

   a. Each of us has attempted to answer this question for himself.

      1.) You know where and how you have been seeking happiness.

      2.) You also know, that although you have often experienced pleasure, true and lasting happiness continues to elude you.

   b. Perhaps it seems that the quest for happiness will never be completely satisfied.

      1.) No matter where we have looked we have not found perfect happiness.

      2.) We might ask if nature or nature's God has played a joke on us by giving us this human desire for happiness.

II Happiness consists in seeking to know and to fulfill the Will of God.

A. Happiness consists in seeking to know the Will of God.

1. The psalmist sees happiness blessing the life of one who concentrates on God's Law as revealed in Sacred Scripture.

   a. The Law of God announced in Sacred Scripture is the revealed Will of God for the direction of human life.

   b. Happiness is intensified by meditation on Sacred Scripture.

      1.) The prayerful consideration of Sacred Scripture leads

to a better understanding of God's revealed Will.

    2.) In meditation one begins to see how the Scriptures can be applied to the circumstances of life.

  2. Using poetic imagery, the psalmist compares the good or happy person to a tree near running water.

    a. Just as the water nourishes the tree, so does the reading of Sacred Scripture nourish the soul.

    b. Just as the tree planted near water does not wither, but grows and produces fruit, so the soul nourished by the Scriptures grows and produces the fruit of holiness.

B. Happiness is found in fulfilling the Will of God.

  1. Happiness is a state of contentment and security.

  2. Contentment and security are achieved by doing the Will of God.

    a. In the poetic imagery used by the psalmist the tree stands tall and strong as it bears fruit.

      1.) Natural storms cannot destroy the tree.

      2.) Its fruit remains on its branches.

    b. The knowledge that one is doing the Will of God brings contentment and security.

      1.) The person doing the Will of God has no fear of human opinion.

      2.) Doing the Will of God is its own satisfaction.

Conclusion: "Happy the man who . . . delights in the law of the Lord and meditates on his law day and night" (Ps. 1:2).

FRIDAY AFTER ASH WEDNESDAY

Introduction: During Lent the Church asks us to perfect the virtue of contrition. Several times during the penitential season Psalm 51 appears in the liturgy to enlarge our knowledge of true contrition. During the course of our Lenten homilies we shall have opportunity to examine in detail the qualities of this virtue. Today we shall consider the first lesson that Psalm 51 teaches us about the virtue of contrition.

I True contrition begins with the admission that one has sinned against God.

  A. True contrition begins with the admission of one's guilt for sin.

1. In Psalm 51 David admitted his guilt.
    a. "For I acknowledge my offense, and my sin is before me always" (Ps. 51:5).
    b. David himself was alert to the fact that he had sinned.
        1.) Although this knowledge caused David pain and distress, he readily admitted his wrongdoing.
        2.) David by his admission took the first step toward perfect contrition.
2. This lesson can be applied to our lives.
    a. The virtue of contrition is the breaking of the will's attachment to persons, places, and things that are opposed to God.
    b. Before one can break these bonds he must admit that they exist and that he is bound by them.
        1.) This is a painful admission.
        2.) Yet the bonds must be sundered if one is to break a sinful attachment and be contrite.
B. True contrition admits the offense is against God.
    1. "Against you only have I sinned, and done what is evil in your sight" (Ps. 51:6).
        a. David recognized that he had offended God.
        b. David was sorry only for the offense against God; he was not sorry for anything else.
    2. Sin is an act of disobedience against the Law of God.
        a. While another human being may be hurt by our sin, even seriously, the sin is primarily an offense against God's law.
            1.) We are all members of the Mystical Body of Christ; what happens to one member of Christ's Mystical Body affects every other member.
            2.) Sin committed by one member of Christ's Church affects the spiritual welfare of the whole Church.
        b. Sin is the disregard of a divine law; it is this disregard that makes a human act sinful.

II True contrition is a search for the merciful forgiveness of God.
A. David sought the forgiveness of God.
    1. David recognized only the judgment of God.
        a. David saw that God's judgment of his sinful deed was deserved.
        b. He admitted that the sentence pronounced by God was just and holy.

2. David pleaded for divine forgiveness.
   a. "Have mercy on me, O God, in your goodness" (Ps. 51:3).
      1.) David was aware that God in his goodness took the initiative in granting mercy.
      2.) David appealed to the goodness of God.
   b. David used a series of words to describe the depth of his need for the divine forgiveness.
      1.) "Wipe out my offense" (Ps. 51:3).
         (a.) Here is a plea to God to erase or blot out the record of David's sin.
         (b.) The above words could also be a cry for God to cancel the debt David incurred when he sinned.
      2.) "Thoroughly wash me from my guilt and of my sin cleanse me" (Ps. 51:4).
         (a.) David sought to be washed clean of the stain left by sin.
         (b.) David desired to be purified from sin.
B. The virtue of contrition prompts one to seek forgiveness for his sins.
   1. The virtue of contrition is not a negative attitude toward God or life.
      a. This virtue recognizes that God can and does forgive sin.
      b. This virtue does not force a soul to live in a vacuum.
   2. The virtue of contrition is very positive.
      a. It directs a soul to turn to God that it may be forgiven.
      b. It enables the soul to be aware of the greatness of God and of its own smallness.
         1.) The soul that is influenced by contrition does not depend upon itself.
         2.) Contrition heightens one's awareness of his dependence upon God and God's goodness.

Conclusion: Contrition leads us to admit with David: "O God, against you only have I sinned." Contrition prompts the eager request: "Have mercy on me, O God" (cf. Ps. 51:6 and 3).

SATURDAY AFTER ASH WEDNESDAY

Introduction: In these days of the Lenten liturgy the Church gives us an outline to follow as we make our resolutions to practice penance, to pray more fruitfully, and to be generous with acts of charity. To persevere in these good works we need a special prayer. Hence we pray in today's liturgy: "Teach me your ways, O Lord, that I may be faithful in your sight" (Ps. 86:11).

I Every believer wants to be faithful to God.

  A. We all know that we owe allegiance to God.

    1. In baptism the soul was consecrated to God's service.

      a. This service is rendered to God by our participation in the liturgy.

      b. We serve God by performing the duties of our vocation.

    2. We know from experience that our allegiance to God has often been defective.

      a. Because of our weakness and personal limitations we have failed.

      b. Frequently we have forgotten the loyalty we owe God.

  B. We pray, asking God for the gift of fidelity.

    1. We make the Responsorial Psalm for today's Mass our personal prayer.

      a. We open our minds so that God may enlighten us with his truth.

      b. We open our hearts so that they may be filled with the love of God.

    2. Like the psalmist we know that those who are filled with the knowledge of and love for God will be faithful.

      a. "Teach me your way, O Lord" (Ps. 86:11).

        1.) In Sacred Scripture "the way" frequently means a manner of conduct.

        2.) Knowing perfectly God's wishes for our lives, we pray for the grace to fulfill his design for us.

      b. We ask for a greater love for God so that we will be constant in serving him and eager to live more completely for him.

II Knowing ourselves and knowing God, we are confident that he will hear us.

  A. Like the psalmist we know ourselves.

    1. Like the psalmist we are poor and afflicted (cf. Ps. 86:1).

      a. A poor man knows he is dependent upon another.

        1.) The poor man pleads for the things he needs.

        2.) In our poverty we stand before God; we pray to him

for everything, in particular for the gift of fidelity.
b. We admit that we are afflicted by weakness.
2. We stand before God dependent upon him and in need of his healing power so that we may remain loyal to him.
B. We know God will answer our prayer.
1. We trust God's mercy.
a. God has promised to answer our prayers, and we know his promises are always kept.
b. We know that God is merciful and kind and will not reject our sincere prayer.
2. With confidence in God we abandon our selfish ways.
a. No longer will we trust ourselves or human judgment.
b. We are confident that we will not be abandoned by God or disappointed by him.

Conclusion: Because weus are poor and afflicted, God will teach us his ways; he will sustain our lives. We will be faithful in his sight (cf. Ps. 86:1-11).

FIRST SUNDAY OF LENT

Introduction: The first reading for today's Mass is taken from the Book of Deuteronomy, and it describes a very ancient religious rite which was composed of two ceremonies. While the Israelites offered to God a basket of the first products to be harvested, they recited a creed. The offering of these first fruits and the accompanying prayer were joyous expressions of gratitude to God.

I The thanksgiving ceremonies of the Israelites were occasions of great joy.
A. The Israelites expressed gratitude to God.
1. The first fruits of their harvest were offered to God in thanksgiving.
a. The first fruits were sacred to God.
1.) They were taken to the sanctuary and there consecrated to God.
2.) The first fruits represented the entire harvest, which the Israelites considered as belonging to God.
b. After their offering was made, the Israelites used the

remainder of the harvest.

    1.) The harvest thus became a gift from God.

    2.) It was used in a spirit of gratitude.

  2. The recitation of a creed accompanied the offering of the first fruits.

    a. This prayer was a brief account of Israel's history.

    b. It was also an expression of gratitude to God.

      1.) In this prayer God was thanked for the liberation of Israel from slavery to Egypt.

      2.) In the prayer God was thanked for leading the Israelites into the Promised Land.

B. The thanksgiving ceremony at harvest time was an occasion of great joy.

  1. It was a time for the sharing of friendship and happiness.

    a. "And having set them (the first fruits) before the Lord . . . you and your family, together with the Levite and the aliens who live among you, shall make merry over all these good things which the Lord your God has given you" (Deut. 26:10-11).

    b. The thanksgiving ceremony was an occasion for rejoicing with family, with friends, and with the priest who received the offering, for the harvest was regarded as a great blessing from God.

  2. The thanksgiving offering was an expression of a cordial friendship with God, a cause of joy.

    a. The worshiper offered the fruits of the harvest to God.

    b. Symbolically God accepted these offerings and invited the worshipers to dine with him.

II Mass is a thanksgiving offered to God.

  A. Mass is offered to God in a spirit of gratitude.

    1. In the Mass we offer to God the first fruit of salvation, who is Christ.

      a. This does not mean that Christ needed redemption; he was without sin.

      b. The phrase "first fruit" is a metaphorical expression when applied to Christ.

        1.) St. Paul says: " . . . Christ is now raised from the dead, the first fruit of those who have fallen asleep" (I Cor. 15:20).

        2.) Christ, gloriously risen from the dead, is offered at

Mass.

   (a.) He is offered as the first fruit because he was the first to rise in a perfect resurrection.

   (b.) Not only is his resurrection the promise of our resurrection, but it is also the cause of our rising from the dead.

2. Mass is an expression of our gratitude to God.

   a. In union with Christ we offer God the Mass in gratitude for all we have received.

   b. The first fruits of the harvest were offered to God in thanksgiving; we offer ourselves in thanksgiving as the first fruits of Christ's redemptive act.

     1.) As we share the sufferings of Christ, so we will share his glory.

     2.) The Holy Spirit dwells in our hearts because we have been redeemed by Christ.

       (a.) The Holy Spirit continues to bring forth the fruit of virtue in our lives.

       (b.) The Holy Spirit's presence in our souls is the promise of our perfect glory with Christ in heaven.

B. The Mass is an occasion of great joy for us.

1. We participate in a sacred banquet.

   a. In a manner unknown to the Israelites, God invites us to participate in a holy meal.

     1.) Christ, whom we have offered to the Father, invites us to receive Holy Communion.

     2.) "This is my body. Take you and eat" (cf. Matt. 26:26).

   b. To nourish our souls God now gives us in Holy Communion the very gift we have offered to him: Christ his Son.

2. Our lives should reflect spiritual joy because we have attended this sacred banquet.

   a. We have not offered God grains of wheat or the fruit of trees; rather we have offered him his Son.

   b. We share with Christ a meal not of cereal nor wine nor fruit, but of his own sacred body and blood.

Conclusion: Rejoicing we thank God for what he has done for us. He has set us free not from the bondage of Egypt but from slavery to Satan. By signs and wonders God has done this; he has done it by the wonder of his love and by the sign of his Son perpetuated here at Mass.

FIRST SUNDAY OF LENT

Introduction: In the second reading for today's Mass, St. Paul wrote to the Romans about the necessity of faith: "No one who believes in him will be put to shame. Here there is no difference between Jew and Greek: all have the same Lord, rich in mercy toward all who call upon him" (Rom. 10:11-12).

St. Paul described the nature of faith when he wrote: "For if you confess with your lips that Jesus is Lord, and believe in your heart that God raised him from the dead, you will be saved" (Rom. 10:9). Here St. Paul explained the act of faith. To "believe in your heart" was to accept the Word of God. To "confess with your lips" was to give an external expression of one's faith in the Word of God by one's manner of life.

I Faith was necessary for the salvation of the Israelites.
  A. In the Old Testament, "faith" had the meaning of "firmness" or "to be true."
    1. The Israelites were to believe in God.
      a. They were to place their faith in God because he was dependable.
        1.) The Israelites were to accept the Word of God because he was stable and not subject to change.
        2.) God had always been true, i.e., faithful to his word.
      b. God had proved in Israel's history that his love for his Chosen People was genuine.
        1.) God could always be depended upon to act according to his word.
        2.) God had always acted in the best interests of Israel.
    2. Faith in God was a source of security for Israel.
      a. When Israel placed its faith in God, he formed a personal association with the nation.
      b. Israel could rest in God.
  B. Faith in God had practical consequences in the life of the Israelites.
    1. The Israelites were to accept Promises made by God.
      a. With confidence Israel was to accept the Will and power of God to fulfill the Promises.
      b. Israel was to dedicate itself to God, both as a nation and as individuals, because God was dependable.

2. Faith in God was the life blood of the nation.
   a. Their faith in God was to nourish the Israelites during that hungry period of the nation's history, the Exile.
   b. Devout Israelites were convinced that God would deliver the nation from every political crisis.
      1.) This faith involved a total dedication to the Will of God.
      2.) This faith required the Israelites to reject the attractions of various political schemes and to place their security in God alone.

II Faith is required for the salvation of the Christian.
   A. St. Paul in today's reading reminds us of the necessity of faith.
      1. The Christian is to accept the Word of God.
         a. God continues to keep his word, sending his only Son into the world.
         b. The death and resurrection of Christ, fulfilling the Promises, continue to be the source of sanctification.
      2. The Christian is to accept the fact that Jesus is the Lord, raised up by God the Father from the dead.
         a. We are to believe that through the death of Christ the Christian is delivered from sin.
         b. We are to believe that through his resurrection Christ gives new life to those who are baptized in him.
   B. Faith requires works of those who believe in Christ.
      1. Faith must be expressed externally by confession by the lips, as St. Paul states.
         a. This is to pray, as we shall today at Mass when we make our profession of faith, or as we do during the day when we make acts of faith.
            1.) The "act of faith" may be the formal prayer we learned at our mother's knee.
            2.) It may also be those spontaneous acts of faith we offer to God during the course of a day.
         b. Faith is expressed in the motive that prompts our activity.
            1.) Faith underlies our awareness of the presence of God as we go about our ordinary tasks.
            2.) Faith spurs us to acts of fraternal charity.
      2. Faith is the total surrender to Christ.
         a. This surrender begins with our baptism.
         b. Surrender continues throughout one's life.

      1.) As this surrender to Christ grows, Christ lives in us (cf.
         Gal. 2:20).
      2.) As this surrender becomes more complete, we die
         with Christ to sin and rise with Christ to glory (cf.
         Rom. 6:4).

Conclusion: "Faith in the heart leads to justification, confession on
the lips to salvation. . . . Everyone who calls on the name of the Lord
will be saved" (cf. Rom. 10:10,13).

FIRST SUNDAY OF LENT

Introduction: Today's Gospel is hard to understand, for in it Our
Lord is subjected to temptation. It is strange that he who was God
would allow the devil to come close enough to tempt him. Why
should Christ, who was without sin, be tempted to sin? Our Lord
permitted this to give us an example of how we, as children of God,
should act even in times of temptation.

I Christ, the Son of God, was tempted in his human nature.
  A. Christ, the Son of God, was tempted.
     1. Christ was the Son of God, as St. Luke states in his Gospel.
       a. St. Luke recorded the miraculous conception and birth of
         Christ.
       b. St. Luke described the baptism of Christ in the Jordan.
         1.) The Holy Spirit descended upon Christ in the form of
           a dove.
         2.) A voice from heaven declared: "You are my beloved
           Son" (cf. Luke 3:22).
     2. After recording these events St. Luke tells us that Christ was
       subjected to temptation.
       a. Full of the Holy Spirit, Christ was led into the desert (cf.
         Luke 4:1).
       b. There in the desert Christ was tempted.
  B. Our Lord was tempted in his human nature.
     1. Christ was tempted to gluttony, to avarice, and to vainglory.
       a. "Command this stone to turn into bread" (Luke 4:3).
       b. "I will give you all this power and the glory of these
         kingdoms . . ." (Luke 4:6).
       c. "If you are the Son of God, throw yourself down from

here . . . his angels watch over you. . . . With their hands
they will support you . . ." (Luke 4:9-11).
2. These temptations were directed to Christ's human nature.
    a. The purpose of the first temptation was to satisfy a human
    need for food.
    b. The second temptation appealed to the human desire for
    wealth, power, and preeminence.
    c. The third temptation was intended to stimulate ostenta-
    tious pride and conceit.

II In conquering these temptations Christ taught us how to live as
children of God.
  A. Christ conquered the temptations.
    1. He conformed himself to the Will of the heavenly Father.
      a. Christ did not act rashly.
      b. Christ prayed.
    2. Christ acted for the welfare of God's kingdom on earth, rath-
    er than for his own purposes.
      a. Christ did not eat to satisfy his hunger; he gave no miracu-
      lous display of his power; he did not dramatically prove
      his divine Sonship.
      b. Christ would wait until the moment appointed by his
      heavenly Father to reveal himself for the good of God's
      kingdom on earth.
  B. Christ taught us how to live as children of God.
    1. We are children of God.
      a. In the sacrament of baptism we received the spirit of
      adoption whereby we became children of God (cf. Rom.
      8:15).
      b. The Holy Spirit dwells in us, witnessing to the fact that we
      are children of God (cf. Rom. 8:16).
    2. We are to follow the example of Christ in times of tempta-
    tion.
      a. God permits us to be tempted so that we may be schooled
      in virtue.
      b. Christ gave us an example of how we can cope with temp-
      tation.
        1.) We can pray, asking God for his help.
        2.) We can always remember our dignity as children of
        God and refuse to degrade ourselves by submitting to
        temptation.

     (a.) Like Christ we are to work for the kingdom of God
        on earth.

     (b.) The example of Christ teaches us not to satisfy
        those selfish instincts that lead to sin.

Conclusion: Each one of us experiences temptation. This should not cause us undue stress. Our Lord was tempted and gave us an example of how to conquer Satan. Following the example of Christ we can say, "Begone Satan."

MONDAY OF THE FIRST WEEK OF LENT

Introduction: Today's psalm should make us change our opinions about the Old Law by which the Israelites lived. Traditionally we think of it as a burden that crushed the Israelites. But today's psalm praises the Law, which is seen as the source of the joy that filled Hebrew hearts with delight.

I The Law and its effects are to be praised.
  A. The Law is to be praised.
    1. The Law is the revelation of God.
      a. Through the Law God reveals his Will to the Israelites.
        1.) Through the Law God gives guidance to the Israelites.
        2.) The Law is perfect and trustworthy.
      b. This revelation is clear and always correct.
        1.) Just as the sun brightens the day, so the Law enlightens the path of the Israelites.
        2.) Because it comes from God, the Law cannot deceive.
    2. The Law dignifies the Israelite who lives by its precepts.
      a. The Israelite who follows the precepts of the Law lives an intelligent life.
      b. Living according to the Law, the Israelite is not debased by the obscene rites practiced by some of his contemporaries in other cultures.
  B. The effects of the Law are to be praised.
    1. The Law refreshes the soul.
      a. The man who searches for God is frequently compared to a pilgrim who is hungry, thirsty, and tired from his day's journey.
      b. The Law brings refreshment to the weary Israelite.

1.) The Law satisfies the hunger of the soul for God.
2.) As the Law comforts the individual and prepares him for tomorrow's tasks, it restores his spiritual energy.

2. The Law rejoices the heart.

a. The Law brings inward happiness and a clear conscience to the Israelite who observes its precepts.

b. The Law instructs and disciplines the Israelite in the service he is to offer to God.

1.) The Law directs the details of the Temple worship which an Israelite offers to God.

2.) The Law is the rule of the daily life of a devout Israelite.

II The Law of God fills our lives with joy.

A. The Law of God gives us joy.

1. As we follow the Law of God our lives improve.

a. By following the Law of God we correct our faults.

b. Success always brings a sense of happiness.

2. The Law of God is a source of security.

a. This Law makes it unnecessary to search for another rule of conduct.

b. God has revealed a rule of conduct in the Law.

B. The Law of God leads us to eternal happiness.

1. The Law of God is a help to eternal happiness.

a. The Law of God is not a penalty.

b. The Law of God is a guide.

1.) We need such a guide because it is impossible for unaided human beings to know the way to eternal life.

2.) The Law of God directs us to a supernatural way of living.

(a.) Unaided human reason could not know how to live in a supernatural manner.

(b.) The Law is a light cast in a practical way on the affairs of daily life.

2. The Law of God describes the discipline we require to reach heaven.

a. The Law of God is a help in controlling our passions so that we may not be led away from God.

b. The Law of God prepares the soul for the influence of the Holy Spirit.

Conclusion: We can make our personal prayer the response for today: "Your words, Lord, are spirit and life" (John 6:63).

TUESDAY OF THE FIRST WEEK OF LENT

Introduction: The Responsorial Psalm for today presents us with a challenge. We are invited to thank and praise God, a task that seems fairly simple. But the psalmist asks us to join him in praising and thanking God at all times. Therein lies the challenge: to thank and to praise God not only when we are filled with happiness but also when we are sick and afflicted.

I The psalmist, David, invites us to join him in his prayer of praise and thanksgiving.
  A. The psalmist offers his prayer of praise and thanksgiving.
    1. We do not know the exact incidents in the psalmist's life that prompted this prayer.
      a. Many commentators on Sacred Scripture find it difficult to connect this psalm to a specific difficulty in David's life.
      b. We do know that the psalmist was afflicted, troubled by some personal anxiety (cf. Ps. 34:5,7).
    2. During a time of trouble the psalmist offered his prayer to God.
      a. The psalmist turned to God, seeking divine help.
        1.) Perhaps his suffering was so intense that he believed God had abandoned him.
        2.) The psalmist indicated he had to search for God.
      b. God delivered the psalmist from his fear and anxiety.
        1.) The psalmist praised God for his help and goodness.
        2.) He thanked almighty God for relieving him of his burden.
  B. The psalmist invites all to join him in a prayer of praise and thanksgiving.
    1. We are among those invited to praise God.
      a. Just as God came to the aid of the psalmist, so will he come to all who call upon him.
      b. We are asked to confess God's supremacy.
        1.) There is no fear that God cannot dispel.
        2.) There is no trial from which God will not deliver us.

    _. We are invited to thank God.
        a. God has shown his unfailing goodness to those who trust him.
        b. We are asked to remember all of God's mercy toward us and to show our gratitude.

II This psalm challenges us to praise God and thank him in the actual moment of trial.
    A. The psalm challenges us to praise God when we are suffering
        1. It challenges us to respect the Will of God in our suffering.
            a. The psalmist insists that what God approves is good, and it is the acceptance of this truth that brings peace, a state of well-being, to the individual.
            b. A respect for God requires honesty in the words of our prayers, but honesty is not a sure defense against sorrow.
        2. This psalm invites all men, especially the afflicted and the poor, to praise God.
            a. "The afflicted" are those who are actually suffering; "the poor" are those who find life too hard to bear.
            b. All who suffer are invited to praise God.
                1.) People who suffer will pray, asking God for relief from their misery.
                2.) The challenge of this psalm is to continue praying, even if God does not immediately grant one's request, and to continue praising him when one is disappointed.
    B. This psalm challenges the sufferer to thank God in the actual suffering that is being experienced.
        1. This psalm challenges the sufferer to continue to thank God for the suffering.
            a. While suffering, one receives the grace to continue to direct his life to God.
            b. While suffering, one should thank God for the experience that is purifying him.
        2. This psalm challenges one to thank God for the pain that is deepening his spiritual experience.
            a. Suffering opens spiritual truths to the individual in pain.
            b. Suffering offers a soul a rich experience of God's presence in the depth of his being.
                1.) One should be thankful for suffering, which teaches the soul that its security rests in God.

2.) Suffering cannot destroy a soul living at an elevated
level of spiritual awareness.
  (a.) The soul at such a level is aware that it will be pre-
  served by God.
  (b.) The soul is aware that there alone is its true existence.

Conclusion: "Glorify the Lord with me, let us together extol his
name.... Look to him that you may be radiant with joy" (Ps. 34:4,6).

WEDNESDAY OF THE FIRST WEEK OF LENT

Introduction: The Lenten lessons on the virtue of contrition continue in the Responsorial Psalm of today's Mass. The psalmist shows
the perfection of his contrition by his sincere prayer for the grace of
conversion.

I True contrition requires prayer for the grace of conversion.
  A. The psalmist prays: "A clean heart create for me, O God" (Ps.
  51:12).
    1. Prayer is necessary for the grace of conversion.
      a. Like all supernatural gifts the grace of conversion can be
      obtained by sincere prayer.
      b. The grace of conversion is the supernatural help one
      needs to direct his life to God.
        1.) Without this divine help the psalmist believes that his
        life would degenerate.
          (a.) He admits he is prone to evil.
          (b.) He asks God to come to his aid so that his
          condition will not worsen.
        2.) The psalmist prays because he has had the experience
        of sin; he knows that he alone cannot direct his life to
        God.
    2. The psalmist asks God to create a clean heart within him (cf.
    Ps. 51:12).
      a. So intense is the psalmist's desire to change his manner of
      living that he asks God to create a new heart for him.
      b. He wants a totally new heart with new desires and new af-
      fections.

B. True contrition requires cooperation with the grace of conversion.

    1. The virtue of contrition is the repudiation of one's former life.

        a. The psalmist is willing to turn away from his former life of sin and turn toward God.

        b. He understands the evil of his sin and realizes the horror of a life without God.

    2. The psalmist prays to God for a new heart.

        a. The psalmist wants a heart that will respond to God's inspiration.

            1.) The psalmist desires to repel every temptation.

            2.) He desires to be faithful in the service he offers God.

        b. The psalmist prays that he will not be excluded from the presence of God.

            1.) He has faith in the mercy of God.

            2.) He lifts up his heart to God, asking that it be purified.

II We pray, asking God for the grace of conversion.

  A. We pray for help.

    1. Prayer acknowledges that we are dependent upon God.

        a. Prayer is the act of an intelligent person.

            1.) An intelligent person knows when he is in need.

            2.) An intelligent person seeks help from one who can assist him.

        b. In prayer we express our need, asking God for help.

    2. We need divine help to change our lives.

        a. We need the divine help to guide us in the proper discipline of our lives.

        b. We need God's help if we are to live in conformity with his Will.

  B. God will grant us the grace of conversion.

    1. God will not refuse us the grace of conversion.

        a. God sent his Son into the world to redeem us.

        b. It would be a contradiction for God to deny us his grace.

    2. God gives us the grace to live intimately with him.

        a. We lift up our hearts to God who fills them with his Holy Spirit.

        b. We leave Mass, and the moments of our personal prayer are renewed.

1.) We take into our work, our homes, and our schools the
graces that fill our hearts.

2.) We can find spiritual refreshment throughout the day
by returning in thought and memory to those moments
of Mass and prayer.

Conclusion: "Have mercy on me, O God, in your goodness. . . .
Thoroughly wash me from my guilt and of my sin cleanse me" (Ps.
51:12-13).

THURSDAY OF THE FIRST WEEK OF LENT

Introduction: The Lenten liturgy encourages us to pray, and to fos-
ter the spirit of prayer in our lives it offers us many examples of
prayer. While the prayers of petition—pleas for God's mercy—are
frequent in the Lenten Masses, other forms of prayer are also suggested. Today's Responsorial Psalm presents an example of the
prayer of thanksgiving.

I The psalmist expressed his gratitude for God's mercy.
  A. The psalmist had experienced the mercy of God.
    1. In a time of trouble the psalmist had cried out to God.
      a. The psalmist had endured some trial.
        1.) He did not describe this trying experience in detail.
        2.) The psalmist expressed his experience in the most gen-
          eral terms: "Lord, on the day I called for help . . ." (Ps.
          138:3).
      b. It is useless to speculate about the nature of this trial.
        1.) Some commentators on Sacred Scripture have stated
          their views as to the nature of the trial or suffering en-
          dured by the psalmist.
        2.) In this psalm there is no evidence to support such opin-
          ions.
    2. God was merciful to the psalmist.
      a. "Lord . . . you answered me" (Ps. 138:3).
        1.) God exercised his power, and the psalmist was freed
          from his trouble.
        2.) God had kept his promise to answer a sincere plea for
          help.
      b. In his mercy God gave the psalmist more than he had

expected.

B. The psalmist expressed his gratitude to God.

    1. The psalmist's soul became permeated with the joyous recognition of God's mercy.

        a. The psalmist admitted that he had been helpless before receiving God's gratuitous gift.

        b. The language of this psalm expresses the psalmist's wonder and awe at God's goodness to him.

    2. The psalmist offered his gratitude to God.

        a. The psalmist's purpose in going to the Temple was to thank God (cf. Ps. 138:2).

        b. The psalmist invited all the kings of the earth to join him in thanking God (cf. Ps. 138:4).

           1.) As the truth of what God had done for him filled his soul with gratitude, the psalmist called on others to help him express his feelings.

           2.) What God had done for the psalmist was evidence of God's mercy toward all nations.

II We offer thanksgiving to God for his mercy.

A. God is merciful to us.

    1. Each one of us has experienced God's mercy.

        a. Although we come from different social, political, economic, and educational backgrounds, we have one thing in common: We know the mercy of God.

        b. In our various life styles, in our different needs, God shows each one of us his mercy.

    2. God is always faithful to us.

        a. He comes to our assistance and forgives our sins.

        b. He helps us in times of trouble.

B. We express our gratitude to God.

    1. As we pray the preface of every Mass, we admit that divine acts of mercy touch our lives.

        a. To the invitation of the priest, "Lift up your hearts," we respond, "We have lifted them up to the Lord."

        b. The purpose of lifting up our hearts, "Let us give thanks to the Lord our God," is realized by the heartfelt expression, "We do well always and everywhere to give you thanks."

    2. We can express our gratitude to God by sharing with others what God has generously given to us.

        a. The Lenten liturgy encourages such works of charity as

sharing our food, our clothing, and our time with those in need.
b. We can share with others the spiritual gifts we have received.
   1.) By our acts of kindness we share with others the goodness God has shown us.
   2.) By forgiving those who have injured us we share the forgiveness we have received from God.

Conclusion: "On the day I called upon you, Lord, you heard me" (Ps. 138:3).

FRIDAY OF THE FIRST WEEK OF LENT

Introduction: It might be said that the Responsorial Psalm for today's Mass is not a prayer for the modern soul. Psalm 130 does express a concern for sin; at the same time it sings of the hope of deliverance from sin. No one can seriously question the modern tension between sin and forgiveness. No one can deny the modern preoccupation with sin and the desire for the improvement of morals. Thus the Responsorial Psalm for today's Mass is truly a modern prayer.

I The psalmist expressed hope for the forgiveness of his sin.
  A. The psalmist expressed his concern for sin.
    1. Aware of his personal sin he cried out to God.
      a. "Out of the depths I cry to you, O Lord" (Ps. 130:1).
      b. The word "depths" is very descriptive of how far the psalmist has fallen from God's favor by sin.
        1.) He recognized the existence of an abyss between himself and God.
        2.) In the poetic expression the psalmist saw himself at the bottom of the abyss calling out to God for help.
    2. The psalmist saw the infamy of sin.
      a. "If you, O Lord, mark iniquities, Lord, who can stand?" (Ps. 130:3).
        1.) Because of sin no one could face God.
        2.) The holiness of God is so overwhelming that the sinner is forced to his knees.
      b. If God, like an accountant, were to keep books or records of human misdeeds, no individual could settle his

account with God.
- **B.** The psalmist expressed his hope for forgiveness.
  - 1. The psalmist compared himself to a night watchman.
    - a. A sentinel kept a night watch over a city or a caravan.
      - 1.) The hours of the night were long and lonely.
      - 2.) Toward the end of the watch the guard would look anxiously at the sky for the first rays of dawn and its promise of relief.
    - b. The psalmist looked to God.
      - 1.) Through the darkness of his sin the psalmist saw the rays of God's kindness.
      - 2.) God alone can forgive, and this divine quality is the reason for respecting God, who is the source of human peace and security.
  - 2. The psalmist was confident that divine mercy would be extended to him.
    - a. "For with the Lord is kindness and with him is plenteous redemption" (Ps. 130:7).
      - 1.) God's love for souls is the reason he forgives sinners.
      - 2.) The infinite power of God is manifested when he draws from the evil of sin the goodness it has buried.
    - b. God's fidelity to his promise stimulates hope.
      - 1.) God has always kept his promise to forgive the sinner.
      - 2.) The psalmist expected God to answer his prayer.

II The Responsorial Psalm for today is a modern prayer.
- **A.** Among moderns there is an attempt to deny the existence of sin.
  - 1. One must say that present-day fashion dictates that we deny sin.
    - a. Today it is fashionable to avoid using the word "sin."
    - b. The word "sin" has a harsh connotation, and its use would expose the hedonistic approach to human behavior expressed in the life style and values of some people.
  - 2. Under this veneer there is a concern with the reality of evil as expressed by the word "sin."
    - a. News media give detailed accounts of the unbecoming behavior of some prominent and not-so-prominent people.
    - b. Indignation is aroused by such subjects as abortion, birth-control, divorce, and the rising crime rate.

B. The Responsorial Psalm of today's Mass is our prayer.
   1. We pray to God, confident he will save us.
      a. Our hope rests entirely upon God.
         1.) From the depths of our misery we cry to God.
         2.) We realize that only God can change the atmosphere
             of evil and moral indifference that we breathe.
      b. Patiently we pray, waiting for God to answer our pleas.
         1.) We know God's unfailing love and mercy for us.
         2.) God will choose the time in which he will relieve us of
             our burdens.
   2. The Responsorial Psalm is an expression of our desire to live
      in harmony with God.
      a. While we share with humanity a common frailty, we
         sincerely turn to God.
      b. Our prayer recognizes that our security is found only in
         God.

Conclusion: ". . . with the Lord is kindness and with him is plente-
ous redemption" (Ps. 130:7).

SATURDAY OF THE FIRST WEEK OF LENT

Introduction: The selected verses of Psalm 119 that serve as today's
Responsorial Psalm are very few in comparison with the whole
psalm. Psalm 119, the longest in the psalter, expresses the spirit of
joy experienced by the soul who has been helped by the Law of
God.

I The devout Israelite was guided by the Law of God.
   A. Through Abraham God had directed the Israelite: "Walk be-
   fore me and be perfect" (Gen. 17:1).
      1. The Israelite was to walk before God.
         a. To "walk before God" means to be conscious of his pres-
            ence in one's life.
         b. The Israelite was to respond to the presence of God by
            complete obedience to the terms of the Covenant.
      2. To be perfect the Israelite was to be totally committed to
         God and to be guided always by the Law of God.
   B. The Law of God was the revelation of God's Will to the Israelite.

1. We must understand what the Law of God meant to an Israelite.
2. Properly speaking, the Law of God was the teaching, the direction, and the guidance that God gave to the Israelite.
3. The Law was the life-giving word spoken by God, and it represented his saving love.
   a. Through the testimonies of his Law, God gave the Israelite rules of conduct, revealing his Will for the nation.
   b. The Law guided the daily conduct of the Israelite through its precepts, which were particular rules requiring obedience.
   c. The ordinances of the Law regulated the association of an Israelite with his neighbor; the person who followed these ordinances was known as righteous before God.

II The Law of God, difficult to observe at times, was a source of joy to the Israelite.
   A. It was difficult for the devout Israelite to observe the Law of God.
      1. The observance of the Law was not free of difficulties.
         a. The psalmist indicates that he experienced some distress and trouble in his efforts to observe the Law.
         b. The piety and devotion of the psalmist was not shared by all of his contemporaries.
      2. The heart of an Israelite was dedicated to learning and loving the Law of God.
         a. There were many things that could distract the Israelite from the Law of God.
         b. Rising above such difficulties, the Israelite proved his love for the Law of God, and in doing so he also proved his love for God.
   B. The Law of God was a source of joy for every soul.
      1. The Law of God was a source of joy for the psalmist.
         a. The psalmist considered himself a pupil who was taught by the Law of God.
            1.) He made every effort to know the Law of God by his personal study of the holy books.
            2.) He committed the Law of God to memory that he might refer to it in all circumstances of his daily life.
         b. The psalmist tested the Law of God.

       1.) He tested the Law of God by his daily experience of
          life in many ways and with many people.
       2.) The psalmist found that the Law was always true, was
          always proved wise.
  2. The psalmist, a devout Israelite, wished to share his joy in the
     Law with others.
     a. The psalmist desired all souls to search sincerely and ear-
        nestly for God's Will in their lives.
     b. As this knowledge grew, the human heart would expand
        with joy.
       1.) The Will of God and the Law of God were one and the
          same for the psalmist.
       2.) Through his Law God was not only directing the life of
          each individual; he was also present to each person.
         (a.) An Israelite would rejoice, knowing that no other
            nation was greater than his nation, which had its
            God so near to it.
         (b.) Through fidelity to the Law, love and joy grew,
            and what was once regarded as a burden came
            to be seen as a blessing; a requirement of the Law
            became a joyful pleasure; and what had been
            thought an obligation came to be considered a
            privilege.

Conclusion: "Happy are they who observe his (God's) decrees, who
seek him with all their hearts" (Ps. 119:2).

SECOND SUNDAY OF LENT

Introduction: The first reading for today's Mass allows us to hear a
conversation between God and Abraham. Although to modern ears
their words may seem strange, they have influenced human history. With Abraham God begins the work of restoring human nature to an image of himself. The full restoration of human nature to
the divine image will be completed when we experience our resurrection.

I The faith of Abraham was the beginning of the restoration of the
  image of God in human nature.
  A. The image of God in human nature was broken by sin.

1. Human nature was created in the image of God.
   a. "Let us make man in our image, after our likeness" (Gen. 1:26).
      1.) Adam was created in the image if God.
      2.) God cast a deep sleep over Adam, and from his rib Eve was formed.
   b. Here in Genesis we have the account of the special creation of the human race, with men and women both made in the image of God.
2. Sin broke the image of God in human nature.
   a. The sin of our first parents destroyed the supernatural image of God in human nature.
   b. After sin, with its loss of grace and infused virtues, human beings could no longer live a supernatural life.

B. With Abraham God began the work of restoring his image in human nature.
   1. God made a covenant with Abraham.
      a. God promised Abraham that he would be the father of a great nation whose members would be as numerous as the stars of the sky.
      b. As in the case of Adam a deep sleep came over Abraham.
         1.) In the darkness God appeared to Abraham in the form of a flaming torch.
         2.) God, in the terms of the Covenant, promised Abraham that his descendants would possess the land.
   2. The image of God began to take form in human nature.
      a. Abraham responded to the promise of God with faith and obedience.
      b. St. Paul speaks of Abraham's reaction to God's words: ". . . he never questioned or doubted God's promise; rather, he was strengthened in faith and gave glory to God, fully persuaded that God could do whatever he had promised. Thus his faith was credited to him as justice" (Rom. 4:20-22).
         1.) Here the word "justice" means conformity with the standard established by God.
         2.) In the faith of Abraham God found what he had not found in Adam.

II Your faith continues the restoration of the image of God in human nature.
   A. The faith of Abraham was a type of your faith.

1. Abraham believed that God would bring new life into the
   world.
   a. Abraham was aware of his and Sarah's physical disability.
   b. Abraham believed that God would give children to him
      and Sarah despite Sarah's barrenness.
2. You believe that God did bring new life, the Risen Christ,
   from the barren tomb.
   a. Because of the resurrection of Christ, you too will rise
      again.
   b. The resurrection of Christ is your guarantee of salvation.

B. Living in faith, you perpetuate the restoration of the image of
   God in human nature.
   1. God's gift of restoration of the human race is given gratui-
      tously.
      a. Gratuitously God gave Abraham the promise and gra-
         ciously fulfilled that promise.
      b. God's restoration of his image in human nature is freely
         given by him through the death and resurrection of
         Christ.
   2. By faith individuals cooperate in the work of restoring the
      image of God in human nature.
      a. Today God requires of us, as he did of Abraham, a faith-
         response to his gift.
      b. Your conviction in faith of your personal resurrection in-
         fluences your life.
         1.) The faith-assurance of new life in Christ influences
             your judgments on material things and helps you to
             sanctify your time.
         2.) Like the Risen Christ you live for God.

Conclusion: All of us, like Abraham, experience the tension of faith
from time to time. May we, like Abraham, never question or doubt
God's promise; rather, strengthened in faith, may we give glory to
God (cf. Rom. 4:20).

SECOND SUNDAY OF LENT

Introduction: Today, it seems, we are greeted by a boastful cry
from St. Paul. Who would dare refer to himself as an example to be
imitated? This is exactly what St. Paul did when he said: "Be
imitators of me, my brothers" (Phil. 3:17). Of course St. Paul could

say truthfully that he was the follower of Christ and that anyone who imitated him would be following Christ. What St. Paul meant is repeated in the invitation of the Preface of the Mass: "Lift up your hearts."

I St. Paul invited the Christians of Philippi to lift up their hearts.
  A. There were some people who were trying to mislead the young church at Philippi.
    1. Persons opposed to St. Paul were advancing alternatives to Christianity, thus causing bitter tension in the church.
      a. Some were advancing a libertine's approach to life; others demanded an immediate return to the Mosaic observance (cf. Phil. 3:2-11 and 17-21).
      b. St. Paul did not offer a positive identification of these individuals, but his Christlike concern for souls impelled him to advise the Philippians of the danger.
    2. St. Paul used very descriptive language to indicate those who would subvert the young church (cf. Phil. 3:19).
      a. "Their god is their belly" refers to certain individuals who indulged their appetites excessively; these people claimed that their god had no concern for their bodies because their worship of a spiritual god was so pure.
      b. ". . . their glory is in their shame" refers to those who claimed that freedom released them from all restraint.
      c. ". . . who are set upon the things of this world." Here St. Paul seems to be using sarcasm, for he is referring to individuals who claimed that their only concern was for spiritual things but whose actions contradicted this claim.
  B. St. Paul exhorted the young church at Philippi to imitate him.
    1. St. Paul was a perfect model for the new Christians.
      a. He was not deceived by the errors that were hidden under the mask of Christianity.
      b. He had lifted up his heart to the truth of Christ and lived it; he was a perfect example of Christian living.
    2. St. Paul insisted that perfect salvation was not achieved here and now.
      a. He referred to the need for a constant striving for salvation (Phil. 3:12ff.).
      b. He asserted the need for personal sacrifice and accepted the judgment which the cross of Christ had already passed on sin.

II The Mass invites us to life up our hearts.

    A. The priest extends this invitation to us at the Preface of the Mass.

        1. The Preface introduces the sacramental celebration of the Paschal Mystery.

            a. The consecration of the Mass is the sacramental celebration of the Paschal Mystery.

            b. We are reminded of the death and resurrection of Christ.

                1.) According to our dispositions these mysteries of Christ are applied to us.

                2.) We are invited to lift up our hearts so that we may know and live the Paschal Mystery.

        2. We are to lift up our hearts after Mass.

            a. What we do at Mass—the lifting up of our hearts—is not confined to the duration of the Mass.

            b. After Mass, when we return to our homes, work, school, social obligations, etc., we are to be people whose hearts are lifted up to God.

    B. The heart uplifted is that which lives as St. Paul lived.

        1. Like St. Paul we are to live in this world.

            a. Here on earth we live in a colony of the kingdom of heaven.

            b. We are true citizens of the kingdom of heaven.

        2. Our real interest should be in our heavenly home.

            a. We lift up our hearts to love and obey our Redeemer-King.

            b. We live with hearts uplifted, waiting for the coming of Christ.

                1.) We know the salvation that he brings transforms humanity.

                    (a.) God created the human body to be glorified, not destroyed.

                    (b.) The physical body is not the cause of human misery.

                2.) Christ will transform us.

                    (a.) Christ will transform us through the power of the Paschal Mystery.

                    (b.) Christ will transform us, and we shall be like him as he is now, resplendent in glory.

Conclusion: St. Paul's invitation to imitate him is not an idle boast.

Like him we are not led astray by the notions of liberty and freedom that translate into moral license. Like St. Paul we lift up our hearts to the Risen Christ and "stand firm in the Lord" (Phil. 4:1).

SECOND SUNDAY OF LENT

Introduction: The Gospel for today's Mass presents for our meditation a unique event, Our Lord's Transfiguration. Peter, John, and James witnessed this marvel, which took place on Mount Tabor according to an unvaried tradition dating back to St. Cyril of Jerusalem. The occasion of the Transfiguration was the prayer of Christ.

I Christ was transfigured as he prayed.
    A. Christ went up the mountain to pray.
        1. Mount Tabor was an isolated place.
            a. The peak of Mount Tabor could be reached with little difficulty.
            b. It was an ideal place to pray.
        2. Christ prayed on Mount Tabor.
            a. We know from St. Luke's account that Christ did pray.
                1.) Christ "took Peter, John, and James and went up onto a mountain to pray" (Luke 9:28).
                2.) We do not know the precise nature of the prayer offered by Christ to his heavenly Father.
                    (a.) St. Luke tells us that while Christ prayed the three disciples fell asleep, an understandable fact when we consider that they were wearied by the climb up the mountain on a summer's day (cf. Luke 9:32).
                    (b.) No doubt this prayer was so personal and intimate that it would be unbecoming for anyone but Christ to witness it.
            b. It would not be doing violence to the sacred text to speculate, that as part of his prayer, Christ asked the gift of understanding for his Apostles.
                1.) Eight days earlier Peter had made a confession of faith, stating that Christ was "The Messiah of God" (cf. Luke 9:20).

2.) But Christ had to teach the Apostles that "The Son of Man . . . must first endure many sufferings, be rejected by the elders, the high priests and scribes, and be put to death, and then be raised up on the third day" (Luke 9:22).

    (a.) It was difficult for the Apostles to accept the idea that the Messiah, Christ, would have to suffer.

    (b.) Therefore it is possible that having made the prediction of his suffering, Christ would pray for the grace the Apostles needed to accept this fact.

B. Christ was transfigured.

  1. The physical appearance of Christ was changed.

    a. ". . . his face changed in appearance. . ."

    b. ". . . his clothes became dazzlingly white" (Luke 9:29).

  2. The physical changes were the effect of Christ's prayer.

    a. St. Luke mentioned the Transfiguration only in relation to the prayer offered by Our Lord: "While he was praying" these changes took place (cf. Luke 9:29).

    b. The Apostles had slept through the prayer of Christ, but "awakening they saw his glory . . ." (Luke 9:32).

II Prayer transforms our lives.

  A. Prayer dignifies the experience of life.

    1. Suffering is dignified by prayer.

      a. Christ went to his crucifixion by way of his Transfiguration.

      b. Prayer keeps our souls strong in the face of adversity.

      c. Prayer releases the grasp of the human heart on the world, and, when the time comes, on life itself.

    2. By prayer we walk the heights of Mount Tabor.

      a. In prayer divine ideals elevate our minds.

        1.) Weak souls can become very strong.

        2.) The discouraged person takes new heart as he realistically faces life.

      b. Prayer changes our life.

        1.) Through prayer the habits of life slowly change.

        2.) Prayer offers us new goals.

  B. Prayer offers the soul the enjoyment of divine consolation.

    1. In prayer the human heart opens to God.

      a. In prayer the heart speaks to God of its intimate desires, its ambitions, and its personal longings.

b. In prayer the human heart is filled with the presence of God.
2. Prayer produces peace and security in the human heart.
   a. Mistrust and dismay disappear from one's heart.
   b. No matter how hidden the hand of God may be in one's life, prayer reveals it.

Conclusions: "Peter said to Jesus, 'Master, how good it is for us to be here'" (Luke 9:33). How good it is for us to be here to pray! How good it is for us to be transformed by prayer!

MONDAY OF THE SECOND WEEK OF LENT

Introduction: In the Responsorial Psalm for today's Mass we read a poetic lament expressing sincere concern for the condition of the Israelites. While Scripture scholars discuss the time and causes of the various assaults on Jerusalem, we do not know to which of those assaults the author of this psalm referred. From it we know that some unidentified enemies had wasted the country, attacked Jerusalem, and desecrated the Temple. The psalmist called upon God to intervene for the nation; he also searched for the answer to the question of why evil exists. Only the fullness of revelation answers this question.

I The poet called upon God in time of trouble.
  A. Great evil had befallen Jerusalem.
     1. There was physical destruction: ". . . they have laid Jerusalem in ruins" (Ps. 79:1).
     2. The religious sensibilities of the people were injured.
        a. "The nations have come into your inheritance; they have defiled your holy temple" (Ps. 79:1).
        b. There was no one to bury the dead (cf. Ps. 79:2,3).
        c. The taunts of the Gentiles, ridiculing the God of the Israelites, were an unbearable humiliation.
  B. The psalmist called upon God to intervene.
     1. God was asked to defend his people.
        a. Only the intervention of God could convince the people of his love for them.
           1.) The heathens dishonored God (cf. Ps. 79:10).
           2.) God's intervention would reinforce his reputation as

the protector of Israel.

b. When God defended Israel his glory would shine before all people; then would all nations be forced to accept his authority.

2. The poet cried to God for vengeance.

a. Today we find it hard to understand such a prayer.

   1.) Today we have the fullness of revelation in the teaching of Christ.

      (a.) From Our Lord's teaching and example we learn fraternal charity.

      (b.) The perfection of fraternal charity, as taught by Christ, requires the forgiveness of injuries and the love of enemies.

   2.) At the time this psalm was written God had not yet presented man with the fullness of revelation.

      (a.) Progressively God made known the fullness of revelation.

      (b.) We should not expect the people of the Old Testament to be aware of what did not come until much later: the fullness of revelation contained in the New Testament.

b. The poet's cry for vengeance can be understood within the context of the revelation which had been made up to the time this psalm was written.

   1.) In the nomadic society of the early Israelites there was no court to which an individual could appeal, nor was there a police force to protect the people.

      (a.) Since the individual could not protect himself, his rights were under the protection of the family or clan.

      (b.) In Hebrew law vengeance was limited to an act that paralleled the injury inflicted.

      (c.) The duty of vengeance fell to the *go'el*.

         (i.) He was a blood relative of the injured person.

         (ii.) It was his function to protect the family from external aggression.

   2.) With this background in mind we can see why God was called upon to avenge Israel.

      (a.) God was considered the go'el of Israel, its next of kin; thus the people believed that God had the obligation to protect Israel.

(b.) This belief rested upon the Covenant by which God had chosen Israel to be his own people.

II The fullness of revelation makes known to us the reason for evil.
  A. The existence of evil does not destroy the goodness of God.
    1. The existence of evil demonstrates the goodness of God.
      a. God could have destroyed evil as soon as it appeared.
      b. God permits evil to exist so that we may freely choose between good and evil.
        1.) If God quickly reacted to evil our lives would be spiritual tragedies.
        2.) God gives us time to realize that we have been wrong, and time to correct our error.
    2. God is so powerful that he can draw the good of our salvation from any evil we may experience.
  B. The fullness of revelation teaches us how to use evil for our spiritual advantage.
    1. Evil can school us in the virtue of fortitude.
      a. We need courage and patience when we come face to face with evil.
      b. When we encounter evil we need perseverance as we wait for God to assist us.
    2. Evil can teach us that we are totally dependent upon God.
      a. In evil situations we are forced to pray to God for his help.
      b. Through the experience of evil we learn our personal limitations and the need to trust God.

Conclusion: As the psalm says, may we, prisoners on this earth, cry out to God for help. We are not seeking vengeance. We stand in need of the mercy of God, who with the greatness of his power will free us. Forever we will thank him (cf. Ps. 79:11,13).

TUESDAY OF THE SECOND WEEK OF LENT

Introduction: Several times in biblical literature God is pictured as convoking a court. In Psalm 50 God is both judge and prosecuting attorney. Individuals are arraigned before him to be judged concerning the dispositions of their hearts at the time they participated in the offering of sacrifice to God. In the judgment it is decided that empty formalistic religion cannot be tolerated in the kingdom of God.

I God convened a court to place on trial the religious attitudes of some people.

  A. God convened a court.

    1. Psalm 50 begins with a herald proclaiming the solemn opening of a law court.

      a. The divine names at the beginning of this psalm represent aspects of God's perfection: the mighty one, the judge, the gracious one (cf. Ps. 50:1).

      b. God had the right to convene this court (cf. Ps. 50:2).

        1.) He had called the earth into being.

        2.) He had established the course of the sun.

    2. Each individual was expected to attend the sessions of this court.

      a. While the delinquencies of some of the Israelites were the special subject of scrutiny, every other human being was also present and was to learn from the proceedings how to worship God.

      b. God was to enlighten the mind and heart of each person present so that he might know from the judgment rendered how to live.

  B. In the verdict of this trial directions for religious worship were included.

    1. The verdict denounced false faith.

      a. The verdict was not directed against the worship of God or the offering of sacrifice to him (cf. Ps. 50:8).

      b. The verdict condemned the false faith of some worshipers of God.

        1.) The condemnation was pronounced against those individuals who thought God was bound to them or that they could satisfy some divine need (cf. Ps. 50:9-13).

        2.) The condemnation also embraced those individuals whose private conduct did not conform to their public profession of faith (cf. Ps. 50:17-20).

    2. The verdict of this court upheld the nature of the true worship of God.

      a. "Offer to God praise as your sacrifice and fulfill your vows to the Most High" (Ps. 50:14).

        1.) The true worship of God was not the presentation of a slain animal at the altar.

        2.) The true worship of God was the offering of a heart

filled with gratitude to God and love for him.

   b. "Then call upon me in time of distress; I will rescue you, and you shall glorify me" (Ps. 50:15).

     1.) True worship of God was the declaration of one's dependence upon him.

     2.) True worship was the offering of sincere prayer in the spirit of adoration, contrition, thanksgiving, and supplication.

II The verdict of the divine court is valid today.

  A. We are to enforce the divine judgment in our lives.

    1. There is no agency that can control or regulate the dispositions of the human heart.

    2. The dispositions of the human heart are very personal and arise from one's awareness of God.

  B. We hasten to participate in the offering of sacrifice to God.

    1. In baptism we were conformed to Christ the priest, and we offer the Mass to God in union with Christ.

    2. We refer to the judgment made by God concerning the offering of sacrifice.

     a. Our participation in the Mass is not an expression of false faith.

     b. Our offering is an expression of our supernatural convictions.

      1.) We prove that our participation in the worship of God is our way of life, for we praise God by our works and manner of life after Mass is over.

      2.) Our charity toward our neighbor is a sign of our love for God.

Conclusion: The verdict of the divine court is most encouraging for us. "He that offers praise as a sacrifice glorifies me; and to him that goes the right way I will show the salvation of God" (Ps. 50:23).

WEDNESDAY OF THE SECOND WEEK OF LENT

Introduction: Could Psalm 31 have been written by an elderly gentleman, a student of life? The conclusion of this psalm, which is not quoted in today's Mass, gives the impression that such a person was indeed its author. His memory was alive, still fresh and green, as he reviewed his life. He reported his experiences and recorded his reactions to them.

No doubt Psalm 31 could be called a universal prayer. People from every age, place, and culture find it an expression of their personal experiences. Christ, dying on the cross, used verse six of this psalm as his prayer.

I The psalmist placed his trust in God when he was troubled.
   A. The psalmist had experienced trials in his life.
      1. The historical background of Psalm 31 is uncertain.
         a. The content of this psalm makes it evident that some personal distress led to the prayer of petition in which God's help is sought.
         b. It is obvious that the combined experiences of suffering and prayer led the psalmist to confidence in God.
      2. The psalmist recorded the trials of his life.
         a. The psalmist was afflicted with physical illness.
         b. Some of his sufferings were inflicted by others.
            1.) Some people had held him up for mockery.
            2.) Others had falsely accused him of wrongdoing and wished to injure him.
         c. His sufferings caused the psalmist some mental anguish.
            1.) In his anxiety the psalmist had the feeling that he was isolated from family, from friends, and even from God.
            2.) The psalmist became apprehensive and used the metaphor of a hunter's net to describe the unknown dangers which could have enmeshed him.
   B. The psalmist expressed his confidence in God.
      1. The psalmist described God as faithful.
         a. God never changed his mind.
            1.) The psalmist recalled that God had consistently extended divine protection and guidance to him.
            2.) The psalmist remembered that God's constant love for him was expressed in the divine justice and hatred of iniquity.
         b. The psalmist remembered that at every stage of his life God had sustained him.
      2. The psalmist placed his life in God's hands.
         a. He prayed that God would save him from the evil around him.

b. The psalmist prayed that God would destroy his enemies.

II We pray to God with confidence.
  A. At times it seems that life has trapped us and we cannot escape.
    1. At times the psalmist's metaphor of the hunter's net seems to describe our situation.
      a. A hunter conceals his net from his prey to catch the unsuspecting animal.
        1.) Unsuspectingly the animal comes to the net which falls over it.
        2.) The net grips the animal, which violently reacts in an effort to free itself.
      b. Unsuspectingly trouble falls on us.
        1.) It can arise from any source or circumstance, or from our own sleeping passions when they are aroused.
        2.) Trouble enmeshes us and violently we attempt to avoid or flee the difficulties.
    2. When troubles come it seems there is nothing we can do to free ourselves.
      a. We try to pray, but our mind seems filled with distractions.
      b. We try hard to solve the problem.
        1.) We use every method we know to control our passions.
        2.) We apologize if we have injured another; we seek reconciliation when a misunderstanding arises.
  B. We turn to God, confident of his help.
    1. Laboring under the burdens of life, we may cry out against life.
      a. The cry, a momentary one, is an expression of our impatience.
      b. The cry is not rebellion against God.
    2. We pause to reflect and to pray to God with trust.
      a. This reflection is the first step to gain control.
      b. We place our trust in God.
        1.) We see God as a friend who is coming to help us.
        2.) We are confident that God will free us from the entanglements of life.
          (a.) In prayer we place our life in God's hands.
          (b.) We are confident God will care for us and will support us in all the events of life.

Conclusion: No matter what the circumstances of life may be, with confidence we pray: "Into your hands I commit my spirit" (Ps. 31:6).

THURSDAY OF THE SECOND WEEK OF LENT

Introduction: Today the Church invites us to listen to a sage of the Old Testament as we pray the Responsorial Psalm. This psalm was written by a philosopher who had a rich experience in the practical affairs of life. He had time to reflect on the details of daily existence. In poetic language this psalmist describes the quality of life that results from one's basic choice of good or evil.

I Human life is characterized by a series of choices.
  A. The vegetable and animal life that surrounds us is determined by the laws of nature.
    1. The life of plants, trees, and vegetables follows predetermined laws of nature.
      a. This type of life develops from a seed and grows to a plant that produces a flower and some type of fruit.
      b. This form of life manifests no self-determination.
    2. The animals of the earth and the birds of the air live according to their natural instincts.
  B. Human life is a series of choices.
    1. Human beings must think about what they are going to do and how they are going to live.
    2. Having considered the options, an individual makes his choice of what seems best for him.
      a. The individual may choose what is contrary to reason or his better instincts or good breeding.
      b. But the fact is he makes a choice; he follows his own will.

II The psalmist teaches that the quality of life flows from the basic choice of good or evil.
  A. A disastrous life results from the choice of evil.
    1. The psalmist shows how the choice of evil grows in the human heart.
      a. First, a person seeks counsel.
        1.) He selects a wicked person as a confidant.
        2.) Then he follows the evil advice he has received.

    b. After a time an individual sits with wicked men.

        1.) He enjoys their company and their conversation.

        2.) He accepts the views and life-values of his wicked companions.

  2. After evil is chosen, spiritual disaster strikes the individual.

    a. He has grown to be a wicked person.

        1.) He is imprisoned by his own evil.

        2.) He is subjected to scorn and ridicule by his fellow citizens.

    b. The life of a wicked person is empty.

        1.) The poetic imagery of the psalmist is most descriptive ". . . they are like the chaff which the wind drives away" (Ps. 1:4).

        2.) The wicked have nothing to offer to God (cf. Ps. 1:5).

B. A successful life results from the choice of what is good.

  1. To choose what is good a person must first meditate (cf. Ps. 1:2).

    a. Meditation is prayer in which a person considers himself in relation to God.

        1.) In this prayer the individual considers the principles of faith.

        2.) From these principles he draws conclusions for the practical conduct of his life.

    b. Meditation is also the habit of listening to the Holy Spirit.

        1.) The individual puts aside the confusion of his passions and emotions and is docile to the influence of the Holy Spirit.

        2.) A soul who listens to the Holy Spirit finds delight in God.

            (a.) A meditative soul may be distracted, but it quickly returns to the companionship of God in prayer.

            (b.) Troubles do not destroy such a soul's conversations with God, for he sees in them an expression of God's Will.

  2. The psalmist uses poetic language to describe the success of an individual who has chosen what is good.

    a. The psalmist compares this individual to a sturdy tree (cf. Ps. 1:3).

        1.) As a sturdy tree has its roots deep in the soil, so the soul of the good person is rooted in God.

        2.) As the sturdy tree is not easily uprooted, so the soul

dwelling in the presence of God is secure.
- b. The psalmist uses the figure of a tree planted near running water to describe a good person (Ps. 1:3).
  - 1.) The tree planted near running water never withers; it always produces fruit.
  - 2.) A soul nourished by meditation is not sterile; it is always engaged in the good works of charity.

Conclusion: The good man is successful. Therefore the wise author of this psalm says of the man who has made the choice of what is good: "Whatever he does prospers" (Ps. 1:3).

FRIDAY OF THE SECOND WEEK OF LENT

Introduction: The Responsorial Psalm for today's Mass is a prayer of thanksgiving. The whole psalm considers the intervention of God in the various historical events of Israel's experience. This psalm also thanks God for his protection of Israel as it grew from a small clan to a nation.

The portion of the psalm we pray today gives a brief account of Joseph's life, which served to encourage the Israelites and teach them the lesson of God's goodness.

I The psalmist encouraged the Israelites as he recalled God's protection of Joseph.
- **A.** The psalmist recalled the life of Joseph and God's protection of him.
  - 1. Joseph had endured many hardships.
    - a. Joseph had been sold into slavery by his brothers and taken to Egypt.
    - b. In Egypt Joseph had been humiliated and subjected to suffering.
      - 1.) Joseph had been falsely accused by the wife of Potiphar, "a courtier of Pharaoh and his chief steward" (cf. Gen. 39:1ff).
      - 2.) Joseph had been severely tested when as an innocent man he was thrown into prison.
  - 2. God had protected Joseph.
    - a. While Joseph was in prison his reputation as a wise man had been permitted by God to gain public attention.

b. In the providence of God Joseph had become an influential man in Egypt.

B. The life of Joseph was an inspiration for the Israelites at a time of great trials.

1. This psalm was written after Israel returned from captivity.

a. Returning from captivity, the nation had to endure many trials.

1.) Homes had to be built and cities reestablished.

2.) The machinery of national life had to be repaired and once again put into operation.

b. The nation needed a hero to whom it could look for encouragement.

1.) In recalling the life of Joseph, the people were reminded that God was always faithful.

2.) Joseph was a hero who had accomplished much for his people.

2. The people could see that God's purpose had been carried out in Joseph's life.

a. Taken to Egypt, Joseph had prepared the way for the immigration to that land of his father and brothers and finally of the whole nation.

b. That Joseph had passed the test to which he was subjected was a sign of God's care.

1.) Israel, subjected to the trials of reconstruction after the captivity, would survive because God cared for his people, as Joseph's life proved.

2.) As Joseph had become a teacher of others, so Israel, by its liberation from captivity, would teach other nations the lesson of God's power and mercy.

II Recalling the events of your life helps you to live a deeper spiritual life.

A. The experiences of one's past life are to be considered in a Christian spirit.

1. The purpose of recalling former experiences is to cull from them lessons adaptable to the present circumstances of one's life.

a. Former events are not to be recalled in a slavish manner.

1.) One must realize that it is practically impossible to recall all the details of any day, month, or year.

2.) A too slavish search into the past can result in spiritual disaster because certain memories can lead one to

become morose or even to despair.
   b. Recalling former events can serve to instruct us.
     1.) Some aspects of these events are not apparent at first glance.
     2.) By recalling such events, new details become apparent and more appreciated.
  2. If one is animated by the Christian spirit, recalling the past leads to spiritual refreshment.
   a. One views life in the light of the Paschal Mystery.
   b. The realization that life has not been wasted becomes apparent.
     1.) The purpose of God is seen in both the good and the bad that one has experienced.
     2.) An individual, realizing that God has educated him in the school of experience, now knows what must be done and what must be avoided.
B. Confidence is characteristic of one who remembers his past in the Christian spirit.
  1. The individual lives the Paschal Mystery intensely.
   a. The individual knows that his life, like the life of Christ, flows from the time of Calvary and rejection to the moment of the resurrection and triumph.
   b. The individual more intimately unites his life with the life of Christ.
  2. The habit of recalling one's former experiences helps to make the goodness of God clear to us.
   a. Now fortified in spirit, an individual is prepared to face life.
   b. Such a person experiences a growth in prayer.
     1.) Now his prayer is characterized by an abiding confidence in God.
     2.) This person notices that praise of God and adoration of God are more frequently expressed in his prayers.

Conclusion: Recalling former events of one's life leads one to sing the praises of God.

SATURDAY OF THE SECOND WEEK OF LENT

Introduction: The Responsorial Psalm for today's Mass is a hymn of praise which embraces sentiments of penance, resignation, and intercession. These sentiments serve the purpose of the sacred poet, namely, to honor God by praising him. This praise of God originates in the psalmist's personal experience.

I The psalmist reminded himself of his duty to praise God.
  A. The duty to praise God arose from the psalmist's personal experience.
    1. God had proved his love for the psalmist.
      a. God had bestowed his benefits on the psalmist (cf. Ps. 103:2).
        1.) God had forgiven the psalmist's sins.
        2.) God had healed the physical ailments which may have been aggravated by the psalmist's experiences in exile.
      b. God had not allowed the psalmist to perish in captivity but had permitted him the joy of returning to his homeland.
    2. The psalmist praised God for his mercy.
      a. The psalmist was intensely aware of God's mercy.
        1.) God is a judge and will punish the evildoer, but the divine anger is transient and the divine mercy eternal (cf. Ps. 103:9-10).
        2.) In God's love for the psalmist was a father's compassion for his child.
      b. In the psalm used in today's Mass are verses that reflect this awareness in a hymn of praise of God.
  B. The psalmist offered himself in praise of God.
    1. The psalmist summoned his soul to praise God.
      a. The word "soul" as used here means more than the spiritual component of human nature.
      b. In the Hebrew of the psalms there was no word that translates into our present English as "soul" or "life."
        1.) Perhaps a better translation of the ancient Hebrew would be "totality," referring to the human essence.
        2.) This would embrace the physical, the psychological, and the spiritual aspects of human life.
    2. The psalmist used his whole being in his effort to praise God.
      a. By using his senses the psalmist learned to know God from the wonders of creation; his physical being sang of God's grandeur.
      b. The psalmist used the faculties of his soul to meditate on

God's goodness and to direct the whole of his human experience to the praise of God.

II Our personal experience prompts us to praise God.
   A. All of us have an experience of God.
      1. Nature leads us to an experience of God.
         a. We experience the grandeur of God as it is manifested in his creation.
            1.) The sky, the sea, and the mountains reflect the immensity and eternity of God.
            2.) The sun and the storms show the beauty and power of God.
         b. We experience God in the healing power of nature.
            1.) We see fear in the eyes of the seriously ill and sorrow in the eyes of his family.
            2.) Through rest, diet, and medicine, nature's healing processes develop, and we notice a change for the better in the patient and great relief in his loved ones.
      2. God has touched the lives of all of us by his mercy.
         a. God shows that he understands our weakness when he forgives us our offenses.
         b. Through the sacraments God unites us to himself so that we may enjoy eternal life with him.
   B. We offer our whole being in praise of God.
      1. Here at Mass our intention is to praise God for his mercy toward us.
      2. After Mass we continue to praise God.
         a. We use our eyes to see God in creation, our ears to hear the Word of God in our conversations with our friends.
         b. We use the faculty of mind to know God and the strength of will to love God and our neighbors.

Conclusion: Like the psalmist we have the experience of God. We cry out: "Bless the Lord, O my soul and all my being, bless his holy name" (Ps. 103:1).

THIRD SUNDAY OF LENT

Introduction: Moses had left Egypt and was in exile in Midian. There he tended sheep for his father-in-law, Jethro. From this

occupation Moses was called by God to the vocation he was to fulfill in the life of Israel. From the first reading of today's Mass we
learn an important spiritual lesson: Hearing leads to seeing when a
soul properly responds to God.

I Moses responded to the Word of God and saw his vocation.
  A. Moses responded to what he heard.
    1. First Moses heard the voice of God.
      a. He was attracted to the burning bush.
        1.) He was leading a flock of sheep to a better pasture.
        2.) When Moses came to Horeb he saw the burning bush.
          (a.) He noticed that the bush was not consumed by the
            fire.
          (b.) Curious, Moses went to see why the bush was not
            being destroyed by the flames.
      b. God called Moses and spoke with him.
        1.) God called: "Moses, Moses" (Exodus 3:4).
        2.) God spoke, identifying himself to Moses.
    2. Moses responded to the Word of God.
      a. Having heard God speak, Moses responded.
      b. Moses offered himself to God's service: "Here I am"
        (Exodus 3:4).
  B. Moses listened and was led deeper into the mysterious ways of
    God.
    1. Moses listened to the Word God spoke.
      a. Moses did not attempt to see, but hid his face (cf. Exodus
        3:6).
      b. God took the initiative and continued to speak to Moses.
        1.) First God revealed himself in general terms to Moses
          (cf. Exodus 3:6).
        2.) In a very general way God revealed his concern for the
          Israelites to Moses (cf. Exodus 3:7-8).
      c. During this experience Moses listened in awe and rever-
        ence.
    2. Having listened, Moses saw the mysterious plan of God.
      a. Moses listened and God revealed more of himself: "I am
        who am" (Exodus 3:14).
      b. God revealed to Moses his vocation among the Israelites.
        1.) God desired to liberate the Israelites (cf. Exodus 3:7-
          8).
        2.) Moses knew his vocation was to lead the Israelites

under God's direction (cf. Exodus 3:10).

II In our spiritual lives listening leads to seeing.

    A. In our spiritual lives it is necessary that we first listen to what God says to us.

        1. We may receive impressions that attract us to supernatural realities.

           a. These impressions can attract any of the five human senses.

           b. These impressions can lead to curiosity or to adoration, either of which may serve to stimulate an awareness of supernatural realities.

        2. Once a soul is prompted to seek union with God, it must listen to the Word of God.

           a. It is necessary to listen to God.

               1.) St. Paul insists that faith comes through hearing (cf. Rom. 10:7).

               2.) Sacred Scripture serves to illustrate this truth.

                   (a.) In the Old Testament there are many examples of souls who were called by God and who listened to his voice, e.g. Abraham, Moses, Samuel.

                   (b.) We are familiar with the New Testament examples of this truth.

                      (i.) The Apostles heard Our Lord invite them: "Come and see" (John 1:38) and "Follow me" (John 1:43).

                      (ii.) Saul was on the road to Damascus when he heard Our Lord call him (cf. Acts 9:4).

           b. The New Testament presents the example of the rich young man who heard Christ address him: "There is one thing more you must do. If you seek perfection, go, sell your possessions . . ." (Mark 10:17-23).

               1.) This young man did not listen to Christ.

               2.) This young man was sad and walked away from Christ.

    B. We are led to seeing, i.e., to faith and understanding.

        1. It is necessary to respond to what we hear from God.

           a. This response should be prompt.

               1.) The Apostles were prompt in giving their response to God's Word, and they were led deeper into the supernatural mysteries.

2.) Our promptness in responding to what we hear from God changes our lives as we leave behind us our sins, our imperfections, the opinion of men, and the natural apprehension of our natures.
b. This response should be a sincere seeking of the source of the voice we hear: God himself.
2. We will see what has been hidden.
a. ". . . no one who comes will I ever reject" (John 6:37).
b. We will enter into the supernatural way of life.
1.) For one who may have lost God, it will be seeing life and oneself in the light of a faith that is just beginning its sincere search for the eternal God.
2.) For others, possessing God by grace, it will be a daily revelation of how, by grace, one can live a more intimate union with God.

Conclusion: Listen. Is God calling you as he called Moses? Be still. Listen and then respond: "Here I am" (Exodus 3:4).

THIRD SUNDAY OF LENT

Introduction: In the second reading for today's Mass St. Paul assumes that Christians are aware of their spiritual descent from the Israelites. Since we are the heirs of the Old Testament, St. Paul writes to us of an Old Testament experience that serves to instruct us. As the New People of God, the Old Testament admonishes us to be on guard and to protect our salvation by a healthy fear of self and an invincible confidence in God.

I The spiritual gifts God gave to the Israelites foreshadowed the spiritual gifts given to us.
A. God gave the Israelites many spiritual gifts.
1. God freed the Israelites from bondage in Egypt.
a. God raised up Moses to lead his people.
1.) St. Paul used the phrase, "all of them were baptized into Moses" (I Cor. 10:2).
2.) This means that Moses united the distinct tribes of the Israelites into one nation.
b. During the Exodus the Israelites passed through the Red Sea and escaped from the Pharaoh.

2. God protected the Israelites on their journey through the desert.
  a. God protected the Israelites by a cloud.
  b. God nourished the Israelites during the desert journey.
    1.) God sent them manna.
    2.) God refreshed them with the water from the rock.
B. The gifts given by God to the Israelites in the desert foreshadowed our sacraments of Baptism and Holy Eucharist.
  1. The sacrament of Baptism was foreshadowed.
    a. In the sacramental water of Baptism we are freed from the bondage of Satan and sin.
    b. Although there are many differences among us, through the sacrament of Baptism we are united with Christ and become the New People of God.
  2. The sacrament of the Holy Eucharist was foreshadowed.
    a. The presence of God among the Israelites was symbolized by the cloud and the rock; the Holy Eucharist is the real presence of Christ among us.
    b. The Israelites were refreshed by the water from the rock and nourished by the manna; the Holy Eucharist is the source of our refreshment and nourishment.

II Spiritual gifts do not guarantee salvation.
  A. St. Paul reminds us that some of the Israelites did not profit from their spiritual gifts.
    1. "... God was not pleased with most of them, for 'they were struck down in the desert' " (I Cor. 10:5).
      a. Only two, Joshua and Caleb, of the people who left Egypt entered Canaan, the Promised Land.
      b. The rest of the nation was punished by God, who required them to roam through the desert until all members of the original generation that had left Egypt had died.
    2. St. Paul mentions the sins that caused the divine displeasure (cf. I Cor. 10:7-10).
      a. The sins that caused the divine wrath were evil desires (cf. Num. 11:4,33f.); idolatry (cf. Exodus 32:6,19); impurity (cf. Num. 25:9); presumption (cf. Num. 21:4-6); murmuring and grumbling (cf. Num. 16:41-50).
      b. However the reading for today lists only evil desires and grumbling.
  B. St. Paul says these things happened as an example for us (cf. I

Cor. 10:6).
1. While we have the perfect spiritual gifts, we are to cooperate with the graces they confer.
   a. We are not to presume that our salvation is assured be-
      cause of these divine gifts.
   b. We are to use the sacraments for the purpose God intends
      when he gives them to us.
2. We will not lose the possession of the kingdom of God if we
   cooperate with the grace of these divine gifts.
   a. We must realize that we are on a pilgrimage to heaven.
      1.) While on this journey we are to accept its hardships
          with patience and fortitude.
      2.) We are to obey the authority of the Church, which
          God has appointed to guide us on this journey.
   b. Living in this way, we are assured of entering the eternal
      kingdom of God, not because of ourselves but because of
      God who is always faithful and merciful to his people.

Conclusion: St. Paul cites for us the example of the Israelites. He
wants us to learn from their history a lesson we can use in our daily
lives. May we learn this lesson and take prudent care lest we fall (cf.
I Cor. 10:12).

THIRD SUNDAY OF LENT

Introduction: Today's Gospel records some of the violent reprisals
the Romans inflicted on the Jewish people because of their
attempts to be free. At the time of Christ it was popular to think of
these disasters as punishment for sin. Our Lord uses these incidents
to teach a lesson: Reform one's life. To reinforce his lesson Christ
uses the parable of the barren fig tree.

I Our Lord teaches that people must reform their lives.
  A. To illustrate his meaning Our Lord uses tragic incidents that
     had occurred not long before.
     1. The fate of the Galileans is a warning.
        a. Pilate had inflicted severe punishment on some of the
           people from Galilee (cf. Luke 13:1).
        b. These people were not the greatest sinners in Galilee (cf.
           Luke 13:2).

1.) The enormity of their suffering was not a sign of evil in their lives (cf. Luke 13:2).

2.) "But I tell you, you will all come to the same end unless you reform" (Luke 13:3).

2. Eighteen people were killed by a falling tower in Siloam (cf. Luke 13:4).

   a. Their death does not mean they were more guilty of sin than others who escaped.

   b. "But I tell you, you will all come to the same end unless you begin to reform" (Luke 13:5).

3. Our Lord repeats the warning to reform in order to emphasize its importance.

B. Our Lord teaches that we have a short time in which to reform.

1. Our Lord uses the parable of the barren fig tree to emphasize this lesson (cf. Luke 13).

   a. The landowner did not find fruit on the fig tree.

     1.) He had been waiting for three years for the tree to produce fruit.

     2.) Now he wanted to cut it down.

   b. The vinedresser asked the landowner to wait one year before destroying the tree (cf. Luke 13:8).

     1.) During that year the vinedresser was to work to cultivate the tree.

     2.) If the tree did not produce fruit during that year it would be cut down.

2. The meaning of this parable is clear.

   a. The urgency of the hour is made plain.

     1.) The time of grace is short.

     2.) One must produce spiritual fruit, the works of virtue, before the time of salvation runs out.

   b. Souls must reform in order to produce the fruit of salvation.

II St. Paul understands the nature of the reform Christ desires.

A. Certainly there is no demand for an inhuman self-denial.

1. Inhuman self-denial depersonalizes individuals.

   a. This form of mortification does not allow us to select the form of mortification we need.

   b. It can lead to greater spiritual harm than the evil it was intended to correct.

2. St. Paul with his insights into the meaning of Christ calls

for a very personal reform of life.
   a. The form of mortification of which St. Paul speaks is the reasonable control of one's instincts.
   b. Faith must enlighten the judgment of reason if asceticism is to be a Christian way of reforming one's life.
B. In the Second Epistle to the Corinthians St. Paul outlines this Christian reform.
   1. St. Paul invites us to follow a two-part program of personal reform.
      a. The negative aspect of this plan is its opposition to giving offense to anyone (cf. II Cor. 6:3).
      b. The second part of St. Paul's plan for reform is very positive: We must make ourselves acceptable (cf. II Cor. 6:4).
         1.) ". . . acting with patient endurance amid trials, difficulties, distresses" (II Cor. 6:5).
         2.) ". . . as men familiar with hard work, . . . conducting ourselves with innocence, knowledge, and patience in the Holy Spirit, in sincere love" (II Cor. 6:5-7).
   2. In our daily lives we can follow the reform urged by Christ and explained by St. Paul.
      a. We must be motivated by a desire to please God.
         1.) As mentioned on Ash Wednesday we are the ambassadors of Christ and must work for him (cf. II Cor. 5:20; II Cor. 6:3).
         2.) Like Christ we must say: "I offer you praise, O Father, Lord of heaven and earth" (John 10:21).
      b. The time for our salvation is the present.
         1.) This Lent is the time of pardon and reconciliation.
         2.) God has allowed us to contact other people so that we may influence them by contributing to their salvation.

Conclusion: To heed the warning of Christ contained in today's Gospel we must be aware that this is the day of salvation. This is the time to cultivate all the virtues. This is the time to produce the fruit of our salvation.

THIRD SUNDAY OF LENT

(This year the priest may select for the Gospel for today's
Mass the reading from John 4:5-42 from Year A.)

Introduction: Speaking to the Samaritan woman at Jacob's Well, Our Lord used the symbol of water to represent the grace of God. Christ also used his thirst as an expression of his desire for souls.

I Our Lord was patient and persevering in his zeal for the salvation of the Samaritan woman.

  A. Our Lord was patient in his zeal for the salvation of the Samaritan woman.

    1. Our Lord was zealous for the salvation of the Samaritan woman.

      a. "Give me a drink," Christ asked the Samaritan woman (John 4:7).

      b. Our Lord used the symbol of his physical thirst to represent his desire for the salvation of this soul.

        1.) In the Greek language the root of the word meaning "zeal" signifies something that is hot or about to boil.

        2.) Although Christ felt a physical need for water, since he was tired from his journey (cf. John 4:6), the whole context of this incident indicates that he felt an even more intense thirst for the salvation of the Samaritan woman's soul.

    2. The zeal of Christ was characterized by patience as he led this soul to faith in him.

      a. Our Lord showed his patience by building on what the Samaritan woman already understood to lead her to faith.

        1.) She understood the daily need for water.

        2.) She understood her marital status.

        3.) She understood that the people of Jerusalem were involved in a religious dispute with the people of Samaria about the proper place to worship God.

      b. Our Lord led the Samaritan woman to faith in him.

        1.) Faith in Christ was just beginning to develop within her when she asked for the eternal water offered by Christ (cf. John 4:15).

        2.) Her faith in Christ grew stronger, and when Christ revealed his knowledge of her marital status (cf. John 4:16-19), she said: "I can see you are a prophet" (cf. John 4:19).

        3.) Finally Christ perfected her faith by revealing himself to her: "I who speak to you am he" (John 4:26).

        4.) She hurried off to share her faith with her fellow

citizens (cf. John 4:28-30).
B. Our Lord's zeal was characterized by perseverance.
  1. Our Lord was willing to overlook the prejudice that separated Jerusalem and Samaria.
    a. Hostility existed between the Jews and the Samaritans.
      1.) Because of the Well the Samaritans claimed a special relationship with Jacob, but the Jews of Jerusalem denied this.
      2.) It was unfortunate but true that in the ritual sense Jews regarded Samaritan women as impure; therefore it was forbidden to drink from any vessel that had been touched by a Samaritan woman.
    b. Christ was willing to ignore this prejudice.
      1.) To save the Samaritan woman's soul he deliberately engaged her in conversation.
      2.) He deliberately asked this daughter of Samaria for a drink of water.
  2. Our Lord persevered in his quest for this soul by conquering hesitations and objections.
    a. The woman of Samaria hesitated to give Christ the water he asked for and raised an objection to doing so.
      1.) She pointed out that he had no bucket and the well was deep (cf. John 4:11).
      2.) She also mentioned that Christ was a Jew and she was a Samaritan.
      3.) She spoke of the religious question that separated Jerusalem and Samaria.
    b. Our Lord took the time necessary to converse with her, answer her objections, and motivate her to supernatural faith.

II Our zeal must be expressed by patience and perseverance.
  A. Our zeal must be expressed by patience.
    1. We cannot recoil in the face of opposition.
      a. Experience teaches us that every worthy effort meets opposition.
        1.) The opposition may arise from vested interests who fear that new ideas may detract from their influence.
        2.) The opposition may arise from ignorance, from not understanding the new proposals; or it may be the form of ignorance that lacks foresight.

    b. We must try to overcome opposition.
      1.) Overcoming opposition from vested interests requires great patience.
        (a.) Patiently we must appeal to the better instincts of those who oppose us.
        (b.) There must be a patient seeking of the common good.
      2.) In the face of opposition arising from ignorance one must patiently explain the truth.
        (a.) This could involve the frequent repetition of the true facts.
        (b.) It could involve the patient explanation of all that is involved in the new proposal.
  2. Our patience must always be characterized by kindness.
    a. Kindness is expressed by consideration of others.
      1.) It is the recognition of their dignity.
      2.) It is the patient attendance to what others have to say.
    b. Kindness is shown in the manner of one's approach to others.
      1.) Kindness is found in the words and phrases used in speaking to others.
      2.) Kindness is shown in our approval of what is good in the observations of others and in our willingness to help when help is needed.
B. Our zeal must be marked by perseverance.
  1. There are always delays in achieving anything that is good.
    a. This is the lesson of experience.
    b. To achieve anything good takes time.
      1.) There is a lapse of time between the formulation of plans and their completion.
      2.) The carpenter, the plumber, the artist, the writer, etc., know that time must pass before they can complete their work.
  2. We must be willing to take and to use the time necessary to achieve our purpose.
    a. This is the reason God gives us time.
    b. We must realize that we cannot rush people into decisions that will change their manner of living.

Conclusion: Like Christ we can be zealous for the welfare of others. But zeal must be patient and persevering. Without patience and perseverance it is fanaticism.

OPTIONAL RESPONSORIAL PSALM FOR THE THIRD WEEK OF LENT

Introduction: Psalm 95, the Responsorial Psalm, which is optional this week, is an invitation to praise God. Probably it was written when the Israelites returned to Jerusalem after the Babylonian captivity. This psalm invites the Israelites to sing the praises of God, and it stresses joy and thanksgiving as the motives for doing so.

I The psalmist invited the Israelites to worship God with joy and gratitude.
  A. The psalmist invited the Israelites to worship God with joy.
    1. The psalmist extended an invitation to the Israelites to worship God.
      a. The psalmist called out to the Israelites: "Come, let us sing joyfully to the Lord" (Ps. 95:1).
      b. This was a courteous summoning of the nation to worship God.
    2. The Israelites were to offer to God hearts filled with joy.
      a. ". . . sing joyfully to the Lord" (Ps. 95:1) is the purpose for which the Israelites went to the Temple.
        1.) Having returned to Zion after the exile, their hearts were filled with joy.
        2.) God had proved that he was Israel's Rock of salvation (cf. Ps. 95:1).
          (a.) All through its history Israel had had an invincible defender, God.
          (b.) Like a rock, sturdy and secure, God had always been ready to help Israel.
      b. An important reason for the joy of the Israelite was: ". . . The Lord is a great God, and a great king above all gods" (Ps. 95:3).
        1.) Again God had proved his supremacy over the enemies of Israel, and once again the Israelites enjoyed the privilege of worshiping in the Temple.
        2.) God's dominion is so extensive that nothing escapes his plan.
  B. The Israelites were called to worship God with gratitude.

1. The reasons for gratitude were found in God's attitude toward the Israelites.
   a. God was their creator to whom they owed everything (cf. Ps. 95:6).
      1.) God made the Israelites and gave them all they possessed.
      2.) Everything in the universe was and is directed and controlled by God.
   b. God entered into a Covenant with Israel (cf. Ps. 95:7).
      1.) By this Covenant Israel was a special nation, God's own people.
      2.) God has guided the Israelites through the events of their history and delivered them from exile.
2. The grateful worship of God extended beyond the service offered in the Temple and entered everyday life.
   a. The worship of God in the Temple was not to be an empty service.
      1.) The ceremonies performed in the Temple were to be offered in recognition of God's supremacy.
      2.) They were to be offered with heartfelt joy and gratitude.
   b. The worship of God was offered daily in a spirit of loyalty and obedience.
      1.) The recent experience of the Exile was a warning against carelessness or a too easy confidence in Israel's privileges as God's Chosen One.
      2.) Loyalty and obedience were to be the characteristics of the Israelites' worship of God "today," i.e. day by day (cf. Ps. 95:8-9).

II We are to serve God with joy and gratitude.
   A. To some of our people it seems impossible to worship God with joy and gratitude.
      1. Certain social and economic conditions make joyful and grateful service of God difficult.
         a. The man who has a family and is out of work carries a great burden.
         b. A woman who is faced with housework all day long and one of whose children may be sick, with another in trouble with the police, will find it difficult to be joyful and grateful.

2. But all people, without exception, are called upon to worship God.
   a. As the psalmist called to the Israelites, "Come," so we hear his voice as he summons all of us to the worship of God.
      1.) In addition to the hardships of reconstruction, the Israelites were suffering many anxieties when the psalmist summoned them to worship God.
      2.) We hear this same invitation: "Come."
   b. The soul is stirred to overcome its inertia.
      1.) Some individuals may be willing "just to let things go."
      2.) This invitation, "Come," awakens the soul to praise God.
B. Our joyful and grateful worship of God requires effort.
   1. To be joyful and grateful our worship of God requires thought, practice, and love.
      a. It requires thought so that the individual will think of the good things of life and recall the happiness he has known; in doing so he will realize that these come from God.
      b. It requires practice so that an individual will rise above his present circumstances and frequently think of heaven, recalling that this world is passing.
         1.) It takes time to develop the habit of lifting up one's mind to God and heaven.
         2.) In the preoccupations of life we can serve food, knowing that we are to participate in the heavenly banquet; or put on the children's clothing with the thought that we and they are to be clothed with glory; or remember that God gives eternal rewards for the temporal good we do.
      c. It requires love; love of God, love of family, love of friends must motivate all one does.
         1.) Love changes one's outlook and one's judgment of the circumstances in which one lives.
         2.) It is love that brings joy to all one's actions, aware that Our Lord takes us, our works and our merits, and presents us and them to the Father.
   2. Our joyful and grateful worship of God is expressed by action, holiness, and attention to purification.
      a. Our actions, properly motivated, are the worship of God.
         1.) We offer all our work for the glory of God.
         2.) God has given us many gifts which we use to worship

him.

    (a.) We use our eyes to see the presence of God and his goodness in nature and in every human being.

    (b.) We use our ears to hear the Word of God not only in church but in the conversations we have with each other.

    (c.) We use the faculties we possess to perform the works of charity.

  b. Our personal holiness is achieved in the worship of God.

    1.) We take time to adore God present within us by his grace.

    2.) We converse with God in our own way as we fulfill our duties.

  c. Our worship of God is also expressed by attention to our purification.

    1.) We use the ordinary experiences of daily life to grow in the virtues of patience, humility, love, and loyalty.

    2.) We use the events of daily life to pray.

      (a.) The works of the day suggest to us many intentions for which we can pray.

      (b.) We can request of God by our prayers the various virtues we need to cope with life.

Conclusion: No matter how we may be feeling, or how overwhelmed we are by life's events, or how much we are enjoying the good things of life, we can say: "Come, let us sing joyfully to the Lord; . . . let us greet him with thanksgiving" (Ps. 95:1-2).

MONDAY OF THE THIRD WEEK OF LENT

Introduction: Originally Psalms 42 and 43, which are today's Responsorial Psalm, were one poem of lament. Exactly when the psalm was divided is not known with certainty, but it seems to have been done at an early date to serve some literary or liturgical purpose now lost to us.

    This psalm is the very personal prayer of a very lonely man, but despite his suffering the poet is certain he will possess God. Here is a prayer that can serve the needs of the modern world.

I In his loneliness the psalmist was certain he would possess God.

A. The psalmist was a lonely man who desired to possess God.
  1. The psalmist was a lonely man.
      a. In his psalm the poet did not give us sufficient evidence to help us associate it with a specific historical event or person.
      b. The poet was in exile far from Jerusalem and the Temple where God dwelt.
          1.) Filled with sorrow, the psalmist expressed the frustration and depression that resulted from his inability to reach Jerusalem and the Temple (cf. Ps. 42:7).
          2.) The psalmist felt keenly the ridicule of those who mocked his faith in God (cf. Ps. 42:4).
  2. The psalmist desired to possess God.
      a. The psalmist used poetic language to describe his condition (cf. Ps. 42:2).
          1.) The psalmist identified himself with a thirsty deer.
              (a.) The deer was timid, afraid of natural enemies that could have attacked it as it stood at a water hole.
              (b.) But the deer, thirsty as it was, was driven by the instinct of self-preservation to seek water in another and safer place.
              (c.) The physical suffering of the deer would be relieved when it could drink in safety from a stream of running water.
          2.) The intense desire for God was a thirst in the soul of the psalmist.
              (a.) To the psalmist his thirst was a horrible experience.
              (b.) To the psalmist only the agony of physical thirst could describe his longing for God.
      b. The psalmist longed to experience his former awareness of God's presence and to possess God.
          1.) In the frustration and depression of his exile, the psalmist recalled his earlier experience of the presence of God in the Temple (cf. Ps. 42:5).
          2.) In his memory, the psalmist heard the chant and saw the ceremonial worship of God in the Temple.
B. The psalmist was confident that his desire to see God would be satisfied.
  1. He recoiled from the thought that God had abandoned him.
      a. The psalmist was ashamed at having thought that God

  had abandoned him.
  b. Three times in this psalm the poet mentioned his depression from which faith had raised him so that he was able to live a perfect life of faith.
   1.) He did not seek further explanation of his suffering.
   2.) Faith enlightened him with the realization that God would send divine light and truth to guide him in his exile and to lead him home (cf. Ps. 43:3,4).
 2. The psalmist concluded by calling God "my gladness and joy" (cf. Ps. 43:4).
  a. In his recollection of his former Temple experience the psalmist found reassurance.
  b. He pictured himself once again in the Temple.
   1.) When the psalmist visualized the sacrifice of the Temple, he knew that he would be reunited with God.
   2.) The psalmist saw himself as again united with his people, chanting the praises of God.

II We thirst for God.
 A. Sacred Scripture refers to God as the source of living water.
  1. In the Old Testament, the sacred writers used water as a symbol of God's favor; the displeasure of God is pictured as a flood or a drought.
   a. God is the Creator who controls the flow of water.
   b. God's gift of water to enrich the land was thought of as a divine blessing; a flood or drought that destroyed the land and harvest was considered to be a divine curse, resulting from God's displeasure with his people.
  2. In the New Testament, Christ is referred to as the source of living water.
   a. Christ is the source of living water for us here on earth.
    1.) Christ leads us to God the Father, the Creator.
    2.) Christ quenches our thirst.
     (a.) From Christ flow the divine favors and blessings on the New Jerusalem, the Church, which vivify us, the New People of God.
     (b.) The teaching of Christ is life-giving because it leads us to spiritual refreshment, union with God.
   b. Christ is the Good Shepherd who leads us, his flock, to the perfect pasture, the eternal happiness of heaven.
 B. We who live on earth thirst for God.

1. It is our desire to be united with God that prompts our prayers and works.
   a. To be united with God we pray and attend Mass.
      1.) In prayer we are near God.
         (a.) Sometimes when we pray God seems very far from us.
         (b.) The saints tell us that we are close to God when he lets us experience this remoteness; he permits it so that we may grow in patience, perseverance, and confidence in him.
      2.) At Mass we listen to the Word of God, and we are spiritually refreshed as we apply the lessons of the readings to our daily lives or let those readings influence our outlook on life.
   b. As we perform the works of justice and mercy, we desire to be united with God.
      1.) By these works we imitate the goodness of God.
      2.) Judging correctly these works and our motives as we perform them, we know we are in the presence of God and are led to a more perfect union with him.
2. We want to be eternally united with God.
   a. It is the eternal possession of God that will satisfy every desire and become the source of perfect happiness.
   b. The desire for God sustains us in this life.
      1.) When we experience the trials and difficulties of life, it is the hope of the eternal possession of God that encourages us to continue.
      2.) We think of our moments of joy and happiness as promises of the eternal joy of heaven.

Conclusion: We thirst for the living God.

TUESDAY OF THE THIRD WEEK OF LENT

Introduction: The Responsorial Psalm for today's Mass is very appropriate for modern times. The present inclination to extol the natural judgment of the human intellect and the independence of the human will must pause in the light of this prayer of a humble soul. The psalmist in his supplications remembered his limitations. Appealing to the goodness of God rather than to his personal merits, the psalmist prays for divine mercy and guidance.

I The psalmist prayed for divine mercy and guidance.
   A. The psalmist prayed for divine mercy.
      1. The psalmist knew that he could pray for divine mercy.
         a. God had revealed himself in history and in the Covenant
            as a God who pardoned sinners and saved the afflicted
            (cf. Ps. 25:8).
         b. God always answered the humble soul's plea for mercy.
      2. The psalmist admitted his need for pardon.
         a. The psalmist honestly admitted his failures.
            1.) In his youth the psalmist had sinned by the errors of
               youth's inexperience and carelessness.
            2.) In his maturity the psalmist had transgressed the Law
               by his rebellion against God (cf. Ps. 25:7,8).
         b. The psalmist asked for God's mercy that he might
            become obedient to God.
            1.) Because of God's goodness the psalmist, an admitted
               sinner, was able to retrace the steps of his life.
            2.) By the goodness of God the psalmist would be aided in
               his efforts to live according to the divine Law, which
               regulates human conduct.
   B. The psalmist prayed for divine guidance.
      1. The psalmist asked God to teach him the truth (cf. Ps. 25:9).
         a. He asked God to show him the truth about life, his person-
            al life in particular so that he might please God.
         b. The psalmist wanted to know the true meaning of the
            Covenant (cf. Ps. 25:10).
            1.) The psalmist knew that a knowledge of the Covenant
               would serve to stregthen his union with God.
            2.) The Covenant taught an individual how to live justly,
               i.e., according to the principles of right conduct.
      2. The psalmist sought personal guidance and instruction from
        God.
         a. He prayed to God for knowledge of "the way" (cf. Ps.
            25:4,12).
            1.) The psalmist wanted to know the divine meaning and
               purpose of his own life.
            2.) The psalmist viewed his ignorance of God's plan for
               him as a barrier to salvation.
         b. The psalmist wanted to understand the circumstances

that touched his life.
1.) The psalmist's enemies had isolated him, and his heart was plunged in loneliness.
2.) Only the divine instruction could enlighten him and teach him how to conduct himself.

II We pray for divine guidance and mercy.
  A. We pray for divine guidance.
    1. We are aware that we need divine guidance.
      a. In the complicated circumstances of our national life, the keenest human intellect does not always know the wisest policy to follow.
      b. On the level of daily life the human intellect alone cannot supply all the answers we need.
        1.) Without the help of God we cannot solve the problem of justice in our penal system.
        2.) Without the help of God it is impossible to talk to a hopeless patient in the intensive care unit of a hospital, or comfort a sorrowing parent, or bring happiness to a worthy mother who depends on public welfare for the necessities of life because she has been abandoned by an alcoholic husband.
    2. Our prayer for divine guidance is more than the recitation of words.
      a. Our prayer for divine guidance demands that we hear and learn from Christ.
        1.) ". . . learn from me, for I am gentle and humble of heart," says Christ (Matt. 11:29).
          (a.) Learning from Christ requires us to recognize our need for the supernatural illumination of faith.
          (b.) It forces us to admit that the answers to life's problems are beyond our personal abilities.
        2.) Praying for divine guidance presupposes a willingness to live by faith rather than by the quick answers of worldly prudence.
      b. Our prayer for divine guidance indicates our willingness to discover divine truth.
        1.) At times we must wait patiently to discover the divine purpose which directs all the circumstances of our lives.
        2.) Our prayer for enlightenment is expressed by the

question, "What would Christ do?"
B. We pray for divine mercy.
  1. Our vision must extend to supernatural horizons.
    a. Every solution we propose for the problems facing us must be based on respect for the dignity of each individual.
      1.) The mercy of God grants us the gift of insight into the dignity of each human being.
      2.) The mercy of God prompts our compassion for those who are suffering.
    b. As we use the principles of sociology and psychology and the guidelines of economics, we must be aware of man's supernatural destiny.
      1.) The social and physical sciences make it possible to dispose individuals to the mercy of God, by which each one can achieve salvation.
        (a.) The advance of the physical sciences can remind all people that God is the Creator of the universe, the One who sustains all forms of life.
        (b.) Physical science improves the health and well-being of individuals and serves as a reminder of the better life of the resurrection to which all are called.
        (c.) The social sciences serve to demonstrate the brotherhood of all men and that God is the Father of all.
      2.) All that is good in the human arts and sciences disposes men to God's grace and the gift of eternal life.
  2. We pray that God's mercy will help us to realize that our sins are forgiven.
    a. In an academic way we find it easy to say that God has forgiven us.
    b. We are to become more aware of God's forgiveness.
      1.) It is important for us to realize that our sins are forgiven.
        (a.) Without the awareness that we are forgiven, life becomes an intolerable burden.
        (b.) The knowledge that we are forgiven by God brings us joy.
      2.) The mercy of God makes us aware that our former sins do not now prevent our peace with God.

      (a.) "Peace be with you. . . if you forgive men's sins they are forgiven" (John 20:21,23).

      (b.) "Your sins are forgiven. . . Now go in peace" (Luke 7:48,50).

Conclusion: "Good and upright is the Lord; thus he shows sinners the way. He guides the humble to justice, he teaches the humble his way" (Ps. 25:8,9).

WEDNESDAY OF THE THIRD WEEK OF LENT

Introduction: The Responsorial Psalm in today's Mass is the second of the Alleluia Psalms that conclude the Psalter. These psalms, praising God, were used in the liturgical services of the Temple. In the brief selection of verses from Psalm 147, used in today's Mass, we are called to praise God because of his power and love.

I The psalmist declared that God was to be praised because of his power and love.
  A. The psalmist declared that God was to be praised.
    1. The psalmist repeated what human experience had taught.
      a. It was the excellence of an individual that attracted the admiration and praise of another.
      b. The perfection of God was the reason for praising him.
    2. The excellence of another had to be demonstrated.
      a. The excellence of another was made known by his good conduct and by his skill in one of the arts or sciences.
      b. The excellence of God was made known to the Israelites by his deeds.
  B. God's acts of power and love proved his excellence.
    1. In the history of the Israelites God had shown his excellence by his powerful deeds.
      a. God's power to create proved his excellence.
        1.) God's power was so universal that he could not only create the world and set the course of the stars, but he could also heal a broken heart (cf. Ps. 147:3,4).
        2.) God's creative power controlled ice, sun, wind, rain, snow, frost, and all the forces of nature (cf. Ps. 147:15-18).
        3.) The power of God produced food and cared for each

one of his creatures (Ps. 147:8,9).
- b. God's power in restoring Jerusalem was also a sign of his excellence.
  - 1.) God rebuilt Jerusalem (cf. Ps. 147:2).
    - (a.) He brought the people back to their homeland.
    - (b.) God strengthened the city against attack from its enemies (cf. Ps. 147:13).
  - 2.) God gave the blessings of peace, prosperity, and health to the inhabitants of Jerusalem and to their children.
- 2. God showed his perfection by his love for Israel.
  - a. The perfection of God was shown in the love by which he forgave Israel.
  - b. In his love God treated no other nation as he treated Israel (cf. Ps. 147:20).
    - 1.) To Israel God gave his statutes and ordinances (cf. Ps. 147:19).
    - 2.) God entrusted his revelation to Israel so that it might instruct other nations in the divine Law.

II We praise the power and love of God.
- **A.** We praise the power of God.
  - 1. The praise of God's power requires a change in our attitudes.
    - a. Frequently we attend church and offer our prayers to adore God.
      - 1.) But we consider our attendance at church services and our prayers only as part of our duty and obligation.
      - 2.) The adoration of God must become a part of our daily lives.
        - (a.) An orchard laden with fruit should prompt our adoration of God, for it reminds us of God's goodness.
        - (b.) A field rich with grain aids our prayer of adoration, for we see in this field the Providence of God supplying food for our need.
    - b. The praise of God's power requires that we consider God himself.
      - 1.) We must develop the habit of looking beyond what the eye sees.
        - (a.) Our eye sees the gifts of God.
        - (b.) Prayer of praise considers not only God's gifts but

God himself.

2.) We must see with faith the power of God in creation and in natural phenomena.

3.) We must think in terms of faith that a rich harvest is the result of the divine laws working in nature.

2. The praise we offer God is more than the recitation of words.

   a. Of course we must use words to express our wonder at the visible signs of God's power.

   b. The manifestations of God's power in nature should touch our hearts.

      1.) The greatest praise we can offer God is to use properly what he has given us.

      2.) Our praise of God's power is expressed by our generosity.

         (a.) As we give of our surplus goods to those in need we think of God's power, which has made our gifts possible.

         (b.) When we meet the victims of inequality we should be moved to greater piety, expressing our praise of God who has been so good to us.

         (c.) This piety also praises God by its concern for and charity toward the victims of injustice who, like ourselves, are children of God.

      3.) In referring to nature's manifestations, we frequently use the words "rampage" and "disaster."

         (a.) The course of nature is not only controlled by the power of God but also manifests it.

         (b.) The praise of God requires us to see in faith the divine purpose in nature's moods.

B. We praise the love of God.

1. The prayer of praise flows from our mental habits.

   a. The praise of God's love for us is expressed by our trust in God.

      1.) Our trust in God is the mental habit of looking beyond the trials and difficulties of life.

      2.) We praise God's love by our trust, which sees God's purpose in everyday experiences.

   b. We praise God's love by our joy.

      1.) This joy originates in our realization that God loves us.

      2.) Joy is a mental habit that we cultivate by thinking

frequently of the good things we have experienced and by growing continually more aware that God directed those experiences.
2. We praise God's love when we are eager to bring his grace to others.
   a. We know that God has given us his grace.
   b. We acknowledge that God placed us on earth for some reason.
      1.) God placed us on earth so that we might contribute to the salvation of others.
        (a.) We do this by our prayers for each other.
        (b.) We contribute to the salvation of others by our good example.
      2.) We are to encourage the timid, to comfort the sorrowful, and to be kind and generous to those who are in need.

Conclusion: The praise of God is expressed by our prayers and by our charity toward others. "Glorify the Lord, O Jerusalem" (Ps. 147:12).

THURSDAY OF THE THIRD WEEK OF LENT

Introduction: Earlier this week we considered the Responsorial Psalm that is repeated in today's Mass. Psalm 95 is an invitation to the worship of God, one aspect of which is expressed in the warning: "If today you hear his voice harden not your hearts" (Ps. 95:7). Contrary to what one might think, this warning does not destroy the theme of the psalm: the worship of God. Rather, the warning reenforces the theme.

I The psalmist taught Israel to worship God.
  A. The psalmist taught Israel the reason for worshiping God.
    1. Israel was to worship God because he was "the rock of our salvation" (Ps. 95:1).
      a. The word "rock" is used metaphorically to designate God.
        1.) This word designates God as a sure support, defense, and refuge for the virtuous.
        2.) God is the source of security and strength for the just.
      b. Throughout its history Israel knew the strength of God

and the security he provided for the nation.

2. The Israelites were to worship "the Lord who made us" (Ps. 95:6).

   a. Israel was to recognize God as the Creator.

   b. Israel was, by its worship, to acknowledge its total dependence upon God, who continued to support the nation and each individual.

3. The psalmist also reminded Israel to worship God because "we are the people he shepherds, the flock he guides" (Ps. 95:6).

   a. God was worshiped in Israel because he was recognized as the one who, by his Covenant, led the nation to green pastures and refreshing water.

   b. Israel was the flock God led to salvation through his revelation.

B. The psalmist taught the Israelites how to worship God.

   1. The psalmist called Israel to come into the Temple, into the presence of God, and worship him.

   2. The psalmist described in detail the way Israel was to worship in the presence of God.

      a. The Israelites were to perform certain external ceremonies.

         1.) Israel was to "sing joyfully" and to "joyfully sing psalms" to God (cf. Ps. 95:1,2) as an expression of Israel's joy and thanksgiving upon realizing God's goodness to his people.

         2.) Israel was to "bow down in worship" and "kneel before the Lord" (Ps. 95:6).

            (a.) Bowing and kneeling were postures of respect for God and of homage before him.

            (b.) They were postures that symbolized Israel's fidelity to God.

      b. The Israelites were to worship God by interior attitudes of heart.

         1.) ". . . that today you would hear his voice. Harden not your hearts" (Ps. 95:7,8).

            (a.) The worship of God was an opportunity for serious reflection.

               (i.) The Israelites were to recall their history and avoid the mistakes of the past.

               (ii.) If past mistakes were avoided, the nation

would never again be banished into exile.

(b.) In moments of serious reflection the Israelites would understand the enormity of the stubbornness that had attempted to coerce God into satisfying human demands (cf. Ps. 95:8,9).

(i.) At Meribah the Israelites had quarreled with God (cf. Exodus 17:1-7).

(ii.) At Massah the Israelites had tested God (cf. Num. 20:8-13).

2.) Worship was the obedience of a heart ready to serve God.

(a.) This obedience is to be manifested "today," signifying the promptness and immediacy of the service of God.

(b.) The worship of God was to be shown by a docile heart.

(i.) In the moments of reflection offered by the liturgical worship of the Temple, the Israelites were to listen to God when he spoke to them.

(ii.) Thus Israel would respond to God, and unlike their ancestors, the Israelites would be led by God to his "rest" (cf. Ps. 95:11).

II The Church calls upon us to worship God.

A. The adoration of God by the Church fulfills the biblical notion of the worship of God.

1. Today the Church promotes the communal worship of God.

a. This worship expresses the individual and the communal dependence upon God, who is the Creator.

b. Our revised liturgical worship fulfills the individual and the communal need to express contrition for sin and gratitude to God.

c. Our liturgy expresses the individual and the communal adoration of God.

2. The Church, the New People of God, is selected by God to serve him and to be his witness before the nations.

a. We, the People of God, serve him in the liturgy, and this service is continued in the events of our daily experience.

b. We, the People of God, are witnesses by our faith to the presence of God in the world.

c. By our personal conduct we witness to the divine

goodness, love, and mercy.
B. We worship God by listening to him.
   1. We accept the words of the psalmist: ". . . today you hear his voice. . . . Harden not your hearts" (Ps. 95:7-8).
      a. We listen to the voice of God.
         1.) We listen to God who speaks to us in the readings of the Mass.
         2.) God speaks to us in the teachings of the Church.
      b. We reflect on what we hear from God.
         1.) During Mass we take advantage of the pauses in the liturgy to think about what we have heard in the readings of the Mass.
         2.) After Communion we pause and reflect on what we have just done at Mass.
         3.) In the silence after receiving Holy Communion, we think of the influence Christ has had and will continue to have on our daily actions.
   2. Reflection during the liturgy directs our prompt obedience to Christ.
      a. In our moments of reflection we appreciate all that God has done for us.
      b. Now we are eager to show our appreciation by the way we live.
         1.) Promptly we follow Christ and his law of charity.
         2.) We try to advance the kingdom of God on earth.
            (a.) We are concerned for the foreign missions, but we do not neglect the Church in our own parish.
            (b.) By our prayers and good works we "build up the church" (cf. I Cor. 14:12).

Conclusion: The worship of God fills our lives. In church we hear the voice of God. At home and at work, in school and at a dance or party, we do not harden our hearts against the Word of God.

FRIDAY OF THE THIRD WEEK OF LENT

Introduction: The Responsorial Psalm for today's Mass has been associated with the Feast of Tabernacles in the Hebrew tradition. However, some commentators prefer to connect this psalm with the Passover celebration. But whatever the joyous occasion that prompted the psalm may have been, it called Israel to reflect on God's saving deeds in the history of his Chosen People.

I A joyous celebration did not prevent serious reflection.
  A. This psalm was used by the Israelites to celebrate a joyful occasion.
    1. We cannot answer definitively the question of the origin of this psalm.
      a. It is impossible to determine the exact Hebrew celebration that occasioned this psalm.
      b. For the moment we must be content to say the psalm was associated with either the Feast of Tabernacles or the Passover celebration.
    2. Both the Feast of Tabernacles and the Passover were joyous celebrations.
      a. The Feast of Tabernacles was a joyous celebration.
        1.) It was celebrated at the harvest season.
          (a.) The long hard days of tilling the soil and planting the seeds were over.
          (b.) The people could rest and relax while they enjoyed the fruits of their labors.
        2.) At the harvest time, fruit and grain for the coming year were gathered.
        3.) The Israelites were happy that God had blessed them by providing for their future.
      b. The Passover Feast was also a joyous celebration.
        1.) The Passover celebration commemorated the liberation of Israel from slavery in Egypt.
        2.) The Israelites celebrated not only their freedom but also God's mercy.
  B. Today's psalm invited Israel to reflect seriously on its history.
    1. The psalmist did not cancel the joyous celebration.
      a. The psalmist told Israel, "Rejoice," "Be happy," "Celebrate."
      b. But the psalmist told Israel to know the reason for its joy.
    2. The reason for Israel's joy was found in its history.
      a. In poetic language the psalmist spoke for Israel.
        1.) "An unfamiliar speech I hear" (Ps. 81:7).
          (a.) Before the Exodus Israel did not know God as a savior.
          (b.) God reminded Israel of its deliverance from

Egypt, but Israel did not understand the voice it heard.

    2.) Only after God had fulfilled his promise to free Israel did the Israelites know the saving power of God.

        (a.) God had relieved the Israelites of the burdens imposed by the Egyptians (cf. Ps. 81:7-8).

        (b.) During the Exodus Israel knew the voice of God's mercy.

  b. Throughout its history Israel found its joy in God.

    1.) It was God who supplied every need of Israel.

        (a.) When Israel was burdened God freed the nat'on.

           (i.) God took the baskets of bricks off the shoulders of the Israelites (cf. Ps. 81:7).

           (ii.) God relieved the Israelites of the sacks of seed and the burdens of the planting season.

        (b.) When in its history Israel was in need because of the attacks of its enemies or in sorrow because of the Exile, God showed the people his mercy and love.

    2.) When Israel was obedient to God the people enjoyed peace, prosperity, and security.

II We are to rejoice during the season of Lent.

  A. God calls upon us to reflect seriously on our lives.

    1. The Lenten season offers occasions for personal reflection.

      a. The liturgy for Lent offers us great inspiration.

        1.) Our spiritual lives can be significantly influenced by our reflection on the prayers and readings of the Lenten Masses.

        2.) We can take time to reflect seriously on what we have done and what we have failed to do.

      b. During the Lenten season we are inspired by the doctrine of our redemption.

        1.) The liturgy allows us to hear Christ speak of our redemption.

           (a.) We are confident that Christ died on the cross and rose from the tomb for us.

           (b.) Hearing Christ's familiar voice, our hearts are filled with a desire for eternal life.

        2.) The knowledge that God loved us so much that he sent his Son to achieve our salvation prompts us to love

God in return.
2. During Lent we consider our sins.
   a. We do not try to deny or to defend those past sins.
      1.) Such attempts would silence the voice of faith in us.
      2.) To deny or defend what was sinful would fill our souls with doubts, confusion, and misery.
   b. We consider our past sins with courage.
      1.) We admit our failures and our need for redemption.
      2.) We know that these failures have been forgiven by God's mercy.
         (a.) We are not discouraged.
         (b.) We depend on the grace of our redemption to avoid the same mistakes in the future.
B. Reflection on our lives fills our hearts with joy.
   1. This reflection enables us to follow the counsels of God and not our own advice.
      a. Promptly we turn to God, seeking his help to follow the inspiration of the Lenten liturgy.
      b. We do not stumble along with our personal limited knowledge.
   2. We are joyful.
      a. We know God cares for us and is concerned about our lives.
      b. We know God has lifted from our shoulders the weight of our sins just as he eased the burdens of the Israelites.

Conclusion: The psalmist said: "An unfamiliar speech I hear" (Ps. 81:7). We hear the voice of God. Is it strange to us? Listen to it!

SATURDAY OF THE THIRD WEEK OF LENT

Introduction: During today's Mass the Church asks us to pray Psalm 51 as the Responsorial Psalm. For the third time during the season of Lent we are offering this prayer of contrition to God.

Psalm 51° teaches us that the interior disposition of sorrow for sin

---

°In the outlines for the Friday after Ash Wednesday and the Wednesday of the First Week of Lent the nature of the virtue of contrition was discussed as part of an earlier consideration of Psalm 51.

is more important than any external penitential act performed without this disposition. God did not accept as a sacrifice an animal with a broken bone, but he does accept a person with a broken heart.

I God did not accept as a sacrifice an animal with a broken bone.
  A. Sacrifice was offered to God.
    1. Sacrifice was the offering of some material thing to God.
      a. The offering was made by consecrating the gift to God.
      b. The gift offered to God was later consumed by the individuals who participated in the sacrifice.
    2. Union with God was the reason for offering a sacrifice.
      a. The number and technical names of the sacrifices and offerings of the Old Testament are too extensive to discuss in this homily.
      b. For our purpose it is reasonable to say that the sacrifice was offered either to establish a union with God or to maintain unity with him.
        1.) A gift sacrificed to God signified his dominion over all things.
        2.) Through a voluntary act of sacrifice an individual signified his dependence upon God and his submission to God.
  B. An animal with a broken bone could not be offered in sacrifice.
    1. Animals were offered in sacrifice to God.
      a. An animal was offered as a bloody, rather than an unbloody, sacrifice or offering.
      b. The content of the Responsorial Psalm and the context of Psalm 51 refer only to the bloody sacrifice.
        1.) Cattle, sheep, and goats were the usual victims of bloody sacrifices, but in some cases doves were used.
        2.) The ritual for these sacrifices, generally speaking, consisted of five principal acts.
          (a.) The person making the offering brought the animal to the place of sacrifice to be examined by the priest.
          (b.) The imposition of hands which followed this examination was a sign that the person offering the sacrifice was laying his sins on the animal about to die in his place (cf. Lev. 16:5,10).
          (c.) The animal victim was slain.
          (d.) The blood of the dead animal was received in a dish by the priest and offered by him according to

the kind of sacrifice it was.

   (e.) The remains of the victim were burned on the altar.
2. The animal, the victim of the sacrifice, had to be without defect (cf. Lev. 22:19-25).
   a. An unblemished victim was required because of the sanctity of the liturgical sacrifice.
      1.) The sacrifice was offered to God, who was holiness itself.
      2.) To impress upon the Israelites the holiness of God, to whom sacrifice was offered, nothing associated with the sacrifice could be blemished.
         (a.) The individuals participating in the sacrifice had to be free of any ritual uncleanness.
         (b.) The animal victim of the sacrifice had to be without blemish.
   b. Sacrifice was offered to God by men to expiate their sins.
      1.) To reestablish union with God by this sacrifice of expiation, an animal without defect was the victim.
      2.) The physical integrity of the animal-victim symbolized the desire of the person offering the sacrifice to be integral, i.e., holy.
   c. The sacrifices of the Old Testament promised the perfect sacrifice of Christ.
      1.) Christ, the Lamb of God, was the perfect victim of the sacrifice of the cross.
      2.) The animal-victim of the Old Law had to be perfect.

II God accepts a person with a broken heart.
   A. The human heart is broken by the virtue of contrition.
      1. The word contrition is derived from a Latin word meaning "to crush."
         a. Applied to the role of the virtue of contrition in the soul, the word means that the human heart is crushed by its sorrow for the sins it has committed.
         b. It also signifies that the human heart has broken its attachment to sin.
      2. To say that a heart has been broken by contrition is to acknowledge that our interior dispositions are of prime importance.
         a. Throughout the Old Testament the rite of sacrifice was

the visible sign of man's interior disposition to seek pardon for his sins and to adore God.

b. It is contrition that breaks the obstinate heart and directs an individual to seek union with God.

B. God accepts the offering of our broken hearts.

1. With hearts broken by contrition we come to Mass.

a. We realize that without the desire to adore God, to thank God, to say we are sorry for our sins, and to acknowledge our dependence on God, our presence here is vain and hypocritical.

b. We continue the tradition of the Old Testament as we strive for a perfect interior religion.

1.) Our piety is neither superficial nor self-centered.

2.) Our piety grows out of our daily lives and needs.

2. Here at Mass God blesses us.

a. God accepts the perfect sacrifice of Christ.

1.) Christ was the perfect victim offered to God with intentions that were perfect.

2.) We come to Mass to offer this perfect sacrifice to God, and we try to develop the dispositions of Christ.

b. Just as God accepted the sacrifices of Abel and Abraham, so he accepts our sacrifice.

1.) We offer to God the Lamb of God, God's Son, and we identify ourselves with him.

2.) God accepts our sacrifice and grants us his divine favors.

Conclusion: The psalmist pointed out that God would not accept imperfect sacrifices and holocausts. Today this is still true. Today we offer God our broken hearts, humbled and contrite, a "due sacrifice" with which God is pleased (cf. Ps. 51:21).

THE FOURTH SUNDAY OF LENT

Introduction: Today one hears a variety of excuses for those people who fail to attend Mass when they are not lawfully excused. One also hears the reasons why some people do go to Mass. Some, fearing a mortal sin when they deliberately stay away from Sunday Mass, have only fear as a motive for attendance. Others go to Mass for reasons that are not entirely supernatural.

At Mass today we heard the first reading from the Book of Joshua, and we prayed our response to it by reciting Psalm 34. Both selections, that from the Book of Joshua and that from the Responsorial Psalm, give us a supernatural motive for hearing Mass: gratitude to God.

I The First Reading and the Responsorial Psalm recalled to the Israelites the need to express their gratitude to God.
  A. The First Reading, that from the Book of Joshua, recorded the Passover, a thanksgiving celebration of the Israelites.
    1. The Book of Joshua recorded the celebration of the Passover by the Israelites upon their entrance into the Promised Land.
      a. The Israelites celebrated the Passover upon leaving Egypt, and they celebrated it again when they entered the Promised Land.
        1.) The Israelites' departure from Egypt, the event that began their liberation, was the occasion of the first Passover celebration.
        2.) The Israelites again celebrated the Passover when they entered the Promised Land, the goal of their journey of liberation.
      b. "On that same day after the Passover on which they ate of the produce of the land, the manna ceased" (Josh. 5:12).
        1.) The manna, the food of the Israelites, ceased, thus marking the end of the desert journey.
        2.) The Israelites ate "the produce of the land."
          (a.) This phrase signified the new status of the Israelites.
          (b.) They were no longer nomads of the desert but the owners and caretakers of a land flowing with milk and honey.
    2. The Passover celebrated upon entering the Promised Land was a thanksgiving offered to God.
      a. This Passover was celebrated in a spirit of gratitude.
        1.) The liberation of the Israelites was a great, gratuitous gift of God.
        2.) It was this gift of liberation that completely transformed the Israelites from slaves into free men.
          (a.) The gratitude of the Israelites was their response to this gift of God.

      (b.) The Passover celebration is permeated with wonder at God's generosity.

    b. The celebration was offered to God.

      1.) God alone was the source of the Israelites' freedom.

      2.) God, who had sustained the nation through the many trials of its journey across the desert, fulfilled his promise when the Israelites entered the Promised Land, Canaan.

B. The Responsorial Psalm was also a prayer of thanksgiving.

  1. The psalmist called the humble to join him in this prayer of thanksgiving.

    a. The humble are people dedicated to God, and in some way they have a claim to divine help.

    b. In a humble way the psalmist told his personal experience.

      1.) The psalmist, like many people, was in need.

      2.) In true humility he called upon God, and God delivered him.

        (a.) The psalmist offered his prayer of thanksgiving.

        (b.) He called upon all who have experienced God's goodness to join him in his prayer of thanksgiving.

  2. This thanksgiving prayer contains a challenge.

    a. "Taste and see how good the Lord is" (Ps. 34:9).

      1.) This verse was a challenge to those who hesitated to thank God.

      2.) The psalmist referred to two human senses—taste and sight.

        (a.) Here he asked his audience not to sit about idly, theorizing about God's goodness.

        (b.) By the words "taste" and "see" the psalmist urged his audience to experience the goodness of God.

    b. Acceptance of the psalmist's challenge would have led the Israelites to thank God.

      1.) The Israelites had experienced the goodness of God, but some of them failed to reflect on the experience or to appreciate it.

        (a.) Some of the Israelites took for granted God's goodness.

        (b.) Others grew careless and thoughtless.

      2.) By the very personal encounter with God's goodness and through personal reflection, some of the Israelites would appreciate what God had done for them.

(a.) No one could deny the experience of his senses of taste and sight.

(b.) The Israelites could not deny God's goodness toward them; the indifferent and the careless would grow to appreciate God's goodness if only they would reflect on all that God had done for them.

3.) This appreciation would motivate the Israelites to express their gratitude to God.

II The above-mentioned passages of today's liturgy help us to solve the problem of attending Mass in our time.

A. Both passages solve the problem of our need to participate in the Mass.

1. Many parents ask us who are priests how they can encourage their teenagers to attend Mass.

a. These good people are bewildered by the attitude of some of the younger generation toward the Mass.

b. In seeking the answer to this question, parents enumerate for us priests the reasons given by teenagers for their non-attendance at Mass.

2. One solution is to invite the young person to "taste and see how good the Lord is" (Ps. 34:9).

a. Many say they do not attend Mass because they "get nothing out of it."

b. One has to encourage them to think seriously about God, their need for God, and their need for the Mass.

1.) One should ask in a kind way how a teenager expects to receive something from the liturgy when he does not attend.

2.) If they are not there it stands to reason that they cannot derive any benefit from the celebration of Mass.

c. Remind the teenager of his needs and of how God supplies the needs of individuals.

1.) Perhaps illustrate this by some character trait you have noticed as the teenager moves around the house or talks to a brother or sister.

2.) Appeal to the younger person's need to be accepted by others.

(a.) Insist that one must be aware of his acceptance by God before he can radiate the joy that makes him attractive to others.

    (b.) The teenager has heard criticisms from his peers; show him how God can correct his defects, and that thus being improved, he can and will be acceptable.

B. The First Reading and the Responsorial Psalm for today's liturgy help us to improve our dispositions while attending Mass.

  1. The Mass is our Passover celebration which we offer to God with gratitude.

    a. Christ is our Passover victim.

      1.) Christ died on the cross and rose from the tomb for us.

      2.) Here at Mass we celebrate the Paschal Mystery.

    b. Christ has delivered us from the slavery of sin and the bondage of death.

    c. The Paschal Mystery is celebrated in a spirit of gratitude.

      1.) In the Preface of the Mass we say: "Father, all-powerful and everliving God, we do well always and everywhere to give you thanks."

        (a.) The celebration of the Paschal Mystery begins with this theme of gratitude.

        (b.) The sentiment of gratitude continues as we say: "In memory of his death and resurrection . . . We thank you . . ." (Eucharistic Prayer Number 2).

      2.) At times we say: "Father, calling to mind the death your Son endured for our salvation, his glorious resurrection and ascension into heaven . . . we offer you in thanksgiving this holy and living sacrifice" (Eucharistic Prayer Number 3).

  2. During Mass we express our gratitude to God.

    a. During Mass we "taste and see" the goodness of God.

      1.) We reflect on all God has done for us.

      2.) We know from experience the goodness of God; the celebration of the Paschal Mystery ends with a prayer of praise filled with gratitude: "Through him, with him, in him, in the unity of the Holy Spirit, all glory and honor is yours, almighty Father, forever and ever."

    b. The prayers we hear and those we say during the celebration of the Paschal Mystery are true expressions of our hearts.

Conclusion: God leads us from sin and evil to his grace and life. We come, we taste, and we see the goodness of the Lord. We are grateful.

THE FOURTH SUNDAY OF LENT

Introduction: During this Lenten season we have fasted or performed some other penitential work; we have prayed and attended daily Mass more frequently; and we have been generous in our works of charity. Now as we begin the fourth week of Lent, we may ask if all our efforts have been worth the sacrifice of self and time. St. Paul in the Second Reading of today's Mass answers our question with a confident "Yes." St. Paul tells us ". . . if anyone is in Christ, he is a new creation" (II Cor. 5:17).

I St. Paul sees the death and resurrection of Christ as the dividing line of history.
  A. Here the word "history" is not confined to the recording of world events, together with explanations of their causes.
    1. To us the word "history" includes this definition, but it is much more extensive in meaning.
      a. History is the record of events from the dawn of creation to the present moment.
      b. History, in our usage, embraces the life of each individual and his moral conduct.
    2. The word "history," as used in these pages, includes all activity in this world.
      a. History, as used here, includes both social and cosmic activities.
      b. History, as used here, refers to the relationship of God to the human race and to each individual.
  B. St. Paul views the death and resurrection of Christ as the one event that transforms all activity.
    1. The death and resurrection of Christ are two distinct actions which comprise the mystery of redemption.
      a. Christ died on the cross, and three days later he rose from the tomb.
      b. These two acts complement each other.
        1.) St. Paul says it was "the Lord of Glory" who was crucified (cf. I Cor. 2:8).
        2.) The crucifixion of Christ is his humiliation, and his resurrection is his glorification (cf. Phil. 2:10-11; II Cor.

13:4; Col. 2:15).

    3.) He who died on the cross is the very one who rose from the dead (Rom. 8:34).

2. The Paschal Mystery transforms all human and cosmic activity.

    a. The Paschal Mystery transforms all human activity.

        1.) The old guides for human conduct are no longer applicable, i.e., the Old Covenant is now replaced by the Law of Christ.

        2.) "If anyone is in Christ, he is a new creation" (II Cor. 5:17).

            (a.) St. Paul makes it clear that the redemption of man by Christ is not a mere repair of the human race.

            (b.) God the Father, to whom creation is attributed, wills this work of redemption to change the human race.

            (c.) Christ, cooperating with the Will of the Father, completely changes the human race.

                (i.) The human race, as a result of the Paschal Mystery, now differs from what it was before the Mystery; furthermore, all human activity flowing from this changed race is essentially different.

                (ii.) Each individual must allow himself to be affected by the mystery of Christ's death and resurrection, i.e., the "old man" must be put off, and one must put on the "new man."

    b. The Paschal Mystery transforms all cosmic activity.

        1.) ". . . now all is new," says St. Paul (II Cor. 5:17).

            (a.) This refers not only to man but to all creatures.

            (b.) All things are reconciled to God through Christ.

                (i.) All things are subjected to Christ (cf. Col. 1:13-20; Rom. 8:28-30).

                (ii.) Christ is the head of the universe, and through him all things are sustained in being.

        2.) "Indeed, the whole created world eagerly awaits the revelation of the sons of God. Creation was made subject to futility, not of its own accord but by him who once subjected it; yet not without hope. Because the world itself will be freed from its slavery to corruption and share in the glorious freedom of the children

of God" (Rom. 8:19-21).
(a.) Christ is the exalted head of all creation.
(b.) Through the Risen Christ, cosmic activity will
reach its ultimate goal ". . . that God may be all in
all" (I Cor. 15:28).

II We participate in the transforming action of the death and resurrection of Christ.
  A. We participate in the transforming action of the Paschal Mystery through baptism, by which a person becomes a new
  creature.
    1. Through the sacrament of baptism a person is incorporated
    into Christ and into the Church.
      a. By baptism a person is incorporated into Christ.
        1.) The preposition "into," as St. Paul uses it here, signi-
        fies a movement of the person toward Christ and away
        from whatever is opposed to Christ.
        2.) The movement toward Christ allows the Risen Lord to
        influence the life of a Christian; as a result Christ has
        dominion and influence in that person's life.
      b. By baptism a person is incorporated into the Church.
        1.) Baptism is frequently called the "rite of initiation,"
        meaning that the individual baptized is introduced
        into the corporate life of the Church.
        2.) Through baptism a union with all Christians is formed.
          (a.) "It was in one Spirit that all of us, whether Jew or
          Greek, slave or free, were baptized into one body"
          (I Cor. 12:13).
          (b.) "There does not exist among you Jew or Greek,
          slave or freeman, male or female. All are one in
          Christ Jesus" (Gal. 3:28).
    2. Through baptism a person becomes a new creature.
      a. Through baptism a radical change takes place in the soul.
      b. Once the soul was dead because of sin (cf. Eph. 2:1); now
      after baptism the person is an adopted child of God.
        1.) This adoption as a child of God is accomplished by the
        Holy Spirit communicated to the soul (cf. Gal. 4:6;
        Rom. 8:9, 14-17).
        2.) The Holy Spirit, received in baptism, is the source of
        the Christian's life and conduct; "all who are led by the
        Spirit of God are sons of God" (Rom. 8:14).

B. This transforming action is continued in human life by faith in the Paschal Mystery.

1. Faith is the means whereby a person comes in contact with the Paschal Mystery.
   a. Faith begins with hearing the Word of God.
      1.) Faith is listening to the mystery of our salvation as God reveals it to us.
      2.) Faith is the dedication of self to Christ and to his service in one's vocation.
   b. Faith requires a mind and a heart that are receptive to the Word of God.
      1.) The preparation for this faith removes all prejudice and passion, which could hinder the hearing of the Word of God.
      2.) The preparation for faith is also docility, a willingness to be instructed and corrected by the Word of God (cf. II Tim. 3:16).
2. The transforming action of the Paschal Mystery influences, through faith, the total life of an individual.
   a. The transforming action of faith in the Paschal Mystery influences one's relationship with God the Father.
      1.) As faith develops, a person becomes more conscious of God the Father, not only as his Creator but also as a Father who has accepted that person as a son.
      2.) Faith deepens one's awareness of dependence on the Father.
   b. Faith profoundly affects one's association with others.
      1.) By faith in the Paschal Mystery one is conscious that Christ destroyed the barriers that separate people (cf. Eph. 2:12-14).
      2.) Faith enables one to see all people as children of God who have been redeemed by Christ.
   c. Faith in the Paschal Mystery grows, and the soul experiences a new union with Christ.
      1.) The individual perceives how much God loves him.
      2.) Faith in the Paschal Mystery is the foundation of an ever-increasing love for God.

Conclusion: Yes, our Lenten efforts are meaningful. Our Lenten efforts have an effect in our lives. Our Lenten efforts, motivated by faith in the Paschal Mystery, contribute to our transformation. We are in Christ. We are a new creation.

THE FOURTH SUNDAY OF LENT

Introduction: The Gospel of today's Mass serves to illustrate a theme of St. Luke's Gospel—that God's mercy is offered to all men. With some justification several commentators feel this parable should be named "Parable of the Merciful Father" rather than the more familiar "Parable of the Prodigal Son."

In this parable two lessons are taught; the first is that of the father, who represents God, showing concern for all his children, and the second is that of the response that all must give to the invitation of the merciful God.

I The mercy of God invites all men to enter heaven.
  A. God invites sinners to enter heaven.
      1. Sinners, represented by the younger son in the parable, are invited to enter heaven.
          a. Sinners, like the younger son, take the gifts of God and squander them.
          b. Like the young man of this parable sinners go through life not thinking of the consequences of their actions.
              1.) Sinners, like the younger son, become involved in unrestrained sensuality and extravagance.
              2.) Sinners, again like the younger son, become degraded.
                  (a.) The degree of possible degradation is illustrated in the parable of the young son's taking the work of a swineherd.
                  (b.) To the Jewish people swine are unclean animals, and anyone who tends them is cursed.
      2. In this parable the conduct of the father represents the mercy of God toward sinners.
          a. As the father receives his returning son, so does God receive sinners.
              1.) The father looks for his son; God looks for sinners to return.
              2.) The father goes out to meet his son; God gives the sinner the grace of conversion.
              3.) The father welcomes his son home.

      (a.) The father speaks kindly to his son; God is never harsh with a repentant sinner.

      (b.) The father greets his son with a kiss; clothes him in a robe, the garment of an honored guest; places a ring on his finger, signifying his rank of son with authority in the household; and gives his son shoes, so that no longer is he a barefooted slave but a son in the house.

      (c.) God greets the returning sinner with compassion, and clothes him in divine grace; he restores the sinner to his place as an adopted son of God and to his role in the Mystical Body of Christ.

    b. The father prepares a banquet for his son.

      1.) The joy of a banquet is used frequently in Sacred Scripture to symbolize the joy of heaven.

      2.) God invites the repentant sinner to share the joy of eternal life.

B. God invites those who practice their religion to enter heaven.

  1. Those who practice their religion remain close to God the Father as the older son in the parable remained close to his earthly father.

    a. Such people do not stray far from their church or synagogue, their Father's house, nor do they make unusual demands of God.

    b. Doing what is expected of them, as the older son did what was expected of him, such good people can hope that God will reward them according to his promise.

  2. The mercy of God is extended to people who observe their religious obligations.

    a. God goes out to them as the father in the parable went out to his older son.

    b. The father does not deny the older son his inheritance.

      1.) "All that I have is yours" (Luke 15:31).

      2.) God does not withhold his grace, and it is only the grace of God that sustains anyone in the practice of his religion.

      3.) As the father in the parable invited the older son to the banquet, God invites faithful souls to the joy of heaven.

II People respond to God's invitation to enter heaven, as did the two
   sons in the parable.
   A. Sinners accept the mercy of God and enter the kingdom of
      heaven.
      1. Sinners accept the mercy of God by repentance.
         a. The sinner realizes he has nothing; as the younger son
            wasted his possessions, the sinner throws away his spirit-
            ual goods.
         b. Like the younger son, the sinner "comes to himself" (cf.
            Luke 15:17).
            1.) The younger son in the parable went to work after he
               had squandered his wealth; similarly the sinner may
               for a time try to hide or to deny his condition of spirit-
               ual poverty.
            2.) The sinner realizes that he cannot hide his condition
               from God or from himself.
               (a.) The sinner accepts the grace of repentance.
               (b.) The sinner admits his guilt: "Father I have sinned
                  against you" (cf. Luke 15:21).
               (c.) The sinner returns to God.
      2. The sinner accepts God's invitation and enters heaven.
         a. In the parable the joy of the banquet represents the rejoic-
            ing in heaven upon the return of a sinner.
         b. The sinner, accepting the grace of God with a humble and
            contrite heart, receives the perfection of grace—eternal
            life.
   B. Individuals who practice their religion also receive an invita-
      tion from God to enter heaven, and they must respond to this
      invitation.
      1. In the parable the father invites the older son to the banquet.
         a. The older son responds with anger and hostility.
            1.) In anger this son compares his own fidelity with the
               recklessness of his younger brother.
            2.) The older son attacks the kindness of his father.
               (a.) The older son speaks contemptuously of his
                  brother: ". . . this son of yours . . ." (Luke 15:30).
               (b.) While pointing out that his father had never given
                  a banquet in his honor, the older brother forgets
                  the many good things he has received from his
                  father.
         b. Hurt by the sharpness of this rebuke, the father continues

to plead with his older son to attend the banquet.

2. We who are faithful to the practice of our religion must realize that we need God's grace.

    a. As we reflect on the conduct of the elder son, we begin to
see how like him we are.

        1.) Although we may be scrupulous observers of the
externals of our religion, we may also be motivated by
servile fear or a haughty calculation of our superior-
ity.

            (a.) We may criticize those we see eating meat on
Friday because we ourselves continue to observe
the Friday abstinence rule, but we forget that
those criticized may be doing a more strenuous
penitential work.

            (b.) We may object without reason to the changes in
the liturgy and criticize the Church without love.

        2.) Like the older son of the parable we may speak harsh-
ly of others, forgetting that we are part of the brotherhood of sinners.

    b. The example of the older son in the parable helps us to
leave ourselves open to God's invitation to enter heaven.

        1.) Our faith disposes us to accept God's invitation.

            (a.) Our present fidelity to religious observance is not a
guarantee of salvation.

            (b.) We must continue to strive for the dispositions we
must have if we are to accept the grace of God.

        2.) We are convinced that when we rejoice over the return
of a sinner we do not lose any supernatural gifts.

            (a.) God's goodness to others does not diminish his
love for us.

            (b.) God is free to give his grace to anyone he selects
and at any time.

            (c.) The return of a sinner to God is a constant sign of
God's mercy present in the world.

Conclusion: To saint and sinner God says: "Take the fatted calf and
kill it. Let us eat and celebrate because this son of mine was dead
and has come back to life" (Luke 15:23,24). Let the celebration
begin!

THE FOURTH SUNDAY OF LENT

(This year the priest may select John 9:1-41
for the Gospel Reading.)

Introduction: Physical blindness is a metaphor in Sacred Scripture
for spiritual blindness, the lack of supernatural insight into creation
and human life. The incident of our Lord's healing a man born
blind, recorded in St. John's Gospel, is considered by some commentators and liturgists to be a symbol of Baptism. In the sacrament of Baptism one receives the gift of faith, the supernatural light
of the soul.

I Because of his faith the man born blind was able to recognize
   Christ.
   A. The man born blind received the gift of faith from Christ.
      1. On the sabbath our Lord gave sight to the man born blind.
         a. The purpose of the physical miracle was to teach a spirit-
            ual lesson.
            1.) Christ taught that he was "the real light which gives
                light to every man" (John 1:9).
                (a.) Christ gives both physical and spiritual light.
                (b.) The sin of the man or of his parents, as mentioned
                     by the disciples of Christ, was darkness opposed
                     to the light given by Christ.
            2.) Man will stumble in the darkness of sin, just as a blind
                person may stumble in physical darkness, but Christ
                comes to open the sinner's eyes to the mercy of God.
                (a.) As Christ opened the physical eyes of the blind, so
                     he opens the eyes of the soul.
                (b.) If one yields to the influence of Christ he will see,
                     for only those remain blind who refuse to see.
         b. Christ performed the miracle on the sabbath to teach an-
            other lesson.
            1.) The healing of the physical defect was a sign and a
                promise of the greater healing to take place at the res-
                urrection of the body.
            2.) The sabbath observance would be changed.
                (a.) The original purpose of the observance of rest
                     on the sabbath was to give praise to God for the

work of creation.

    (b.) In the new age inaugurated by Christ's resurrection the sabbath will be the Lord's Day *par excellence*.

    (c.) Christ entered his rest by the resurrection; following him, we have the promise of the eternal sabbath in heaven (cf. Heb. 4:1-11).

  2. The man born blind received spiritual sight and light from Christ.

    a. This man received the gift of faith by which he could see supernaturally.

    b. In the beginning of his new experience of faith, the former blind man knew the name of the Lord and expressed his faith that Christ was not a sinner.

B. As news of this miracle spread throughout the community, the faith of the man born blind was strengthened by the trials he endured.

  1. The news of the cure of the blind man spread throughout the community.

    a. Neighbors who had known the man all is life talked about his gift of sight (cf. John 9:8-10).

    b. The neighbors told the Pharisees about the miracle (cf. John 9:13-18).

  2. The faith of the man born blind was strengthened by the trials to which he was subjected.

    a. We notice the progressive development of this man's faith.

      1.) At first he knew only the name of our Lord: "That man they call Jesus . . ." (John 9:11).

      2.) The former blind man's faith grew through various stages; first, he believed that Christ could not be a sinner because he had worked a miracle; then the man acknowledged that Christ was a prophet.

      3.) As he became accustomed to the light of the sun in his eyes and the light of faith in his soul, the former blind man made an act of perfect faith in Christ: "I do believe, Lord," he said, and bowed down to worship him (John 9:38).

    b. His trials aided the man born blind to grow spiritually.

      1.) First the man was questioned by his neighbors about his cure; he seemed to indicate that he was searching for a satisfactory answer to their question.

2.) The Pharisees subjected the man to severe questioning; they were able to do so because they had a knowledge of Sacred Scripture as well as the authority to expel the man from the synagogue.

3.) Furthermore, the man born blind was sensitive to the embarrassment of his parents, who were questioned by the Pharisees about their son's blindness at birth and his later ability to see.

II Faith, a gift from God, develops through trials.
  A. Faith is a gift given us by God.
    1. God gives us the gift of faith in the sacrament of Baptism.
      a. In the sacrament of Baptism we become adopted children of God.
      b. God gives us the gift of faith that we may be worthy of this adoption.
        1.) Faith, given to us at Baptism, opens our eyes to the supernatural life of grace.
        2.) Faith, given to us at Baptism, is also the supernatural light by which we can see, live, and work as children of God.
    2. God freely bestows the gift of faith on us.
      a. Just as sight was freely given to the man born blind, so the gift of faith is given us by God.
      b. St. John's account of Christ's miraculous cure of the man born blind emphasizes the freedom of Christ to grant the gift of sight.
        1.) "As he walked along, he saw a man who had been blind from birth" (John 9:1).
        2.) When Christ saw the man no one asked Our Lord to perform a miracle, as people had done on other occasions.
        3.) This is a symbol of the freedom with which God bestows the gift of faith.
  B. Faith develops when it is tested.
    1. The personal puzzlement of a believer can contribute to the perfection of faith.
      a. When we question the truths of faith we are able to evaluate them in the light of daily living.
        1.) This is not a denial of supernatural truths.

  2.) It is a seeking for the purpose of learning how, when, and where we are to live by the truths of faith.

  b. This evaluation leads to a greater appreciation of God's revelation to us through the gift of faith.

2. Our faith may be subjected to trials by other people.

  a. People we love or esteem because of their position may question or deny what we believe.

    1.) In such instances our emotions become involved because of the affection or admiration we have for those who question us.

    2.) We are shocked when we hear people we love or admire express their doubts or denials of the faith we profess.

    3.) We face a crisis; we have to make a decision.

  b. It is the personal decision made when faith is tested by others that determines the quality of our faith.

    1.) Our decision can weaken or destroy our faith if the foundation for the decision is only the emotions—love, admiration, and fear of others—that prevent us from being objective in our judgments.

    2.) Remaining sensitive to the opinions of others, we can strengthen our faith if we remain loyal to our supernatural convictions.

      (a.) This requires us to allow our faith to direct our conduct.

      (b.) We make the perfect act of faith when we adore God by a faith that prompts our every action.

Conclusion: Faith is a gift of God that grows when it is the guide of our daily conduct. Trials we may have to endure, but they will serve to perfect our faith.

OPTIONAL READING FOR THE FOURTH WEEK OF LENT

Introduction: Several commentators see Psalm 27, the Responsorial Psalm for today, as a composite of two psalms. The first is considered to be a prayer of confidence and thanksgiving; the other a prayer of lament. Other commentators, following Jewish tradition, point out that the title of the Psalm of David reads, "before he was anointed." This not only dates the psalm at the beginning of Saul's persecution of David but also explains the change in its tone.

The portion of Psalm 27 used as our prayer in today's Mass is an expression of confidence in God who is described as "light" and "salvation" for every individual.

I The psalmist said God was his "light" and "salvation."
  A. The psalmist called God the light of his life.
      1. Frequently, in Sacred Scripture, light is associated with God.
          a. Light is the work of God.
              1.) God is the Creator who called light into being.
                  (a.) Light was the first creature made by God (Gen. 1:3).
                  (b.) God created the lights in the sky to separate day from night—one light to govern the day and a lesser light to govern the night (cf. Gen. 1:14-18).
              2.) In the literary style of the Book of Genesis, God is pictured as separating light from darkness, and the lights God set in the sky were to continue his work of separating light from darkness (cf. Gen. 1:2,3,18).
          b. God is frequently described as "light."
              1.) In Sacred Scripture the inspired authors use the image of light to describe God's glory.
              2.) The inspired authors use light as a literary device to describe the mystery of God's appearances; God is also said to be clothed in light, while his throne is surrounded by light.
      2. God was a light to the psalmist.
          a. In the darkness of his trial the psalmist experienced God as a shining light.
              1.) In this trial the psalmist had lost everything, even the respect of his parents, and he felt keenly his rejection by society.
              2.) During this experience of spiritual darkness, the bright light of God shone in his life.
                  (a.) The psalmist was confident that God would help him and eventually rescue him.
                  (b.) The psalmist remembered the Law of God, and it was the guide of his life during his sufferings.
          b. God's presence in the life of the psalmist was like the sun shining on a clear, bright day.

1.) The psalmist was aware that God was protecting him.

2.) In his trial the psalmist enjoyed a personal union with God who was guiding him by divine mercy.

B. The psalmist said God was his salvation as he waited to be freed from his troubles.

1. The psalmist said God was his salvation.

   a. One meaning of "salvation" is "the taking (of someone) out of a dangerous situation."

      1.) The experience of the psalmist confirmed his conviction that it was only God who could draw him from a dangerous situation.

         (a.) The psalmist had no human help; his enemies were bitter, and he was rejected by his family.

         (b.) God helped the psalmist.

      2.) The psalmist prayed that he would not lose the divine assistance.

         (a.) The psalmist prayed that he would always be acceptable to God.

         (b.). In his prayer the psalmist declared the intention of his heart—to seek only God (cf. Ps. 27:8).

   b. The psalmist prayed with confidence to God, his salvation.

      1.) God had saved the psalmist.

      2.) Now the psalmist wished to remain with God, his refuge (cf. Ps. 27:1).

2. With patience the psalmist waited to be freed from all his trials.

   a. The psalmist understood that God permitted him to suffer.

   b. The psalmist learned great lessons from this experience.

      1.) The psalmist learned to be more confident of God's help because God always saved the oppressed who prayed for divine assistance.

      2.) The psalmist also learned the lesson of patience: "Wait for the Lord with courage" (Ps. 27:14).

         (a.) The confidence of the psalmist is characterized by patience; "Wait for the Lord to rescue me," the psalmist prays to himself.

         (b.) He is certain that with God's help he will be protected from all his enemies and that in God the psalmist will find peace, freedom from trials, and safety from his enemies.

II Christ is our light and our salvation.
 A. Christ is our light who has come into the world.
  1. In the portion of St. Luke's Gospel called the Infancy
  Gospel, Christ is referred to as the light of salvation.
   a. Before Our Lord's birth Zachariah, prophesying, says of
   Christ: "He will shine on those who sit in darkness and in
   the shadow of death, and guide our feet into the way of
   peace" (Luke 1:79).
   b. When Our Lord as an infant is presented to God, Simeon
   says Christ is "a revealing light to the Gentiles. . ." (Luke
   2:32).
  2. Throughout his life Our Lord reveals himself as light for us.
   a. Christ reveals himself as the "Light of the World" by his
   words and his deeds (cf. John 3:19).
    1.) The words of Christ reveal that he is the light by which
    people may live (cf. John 9:5; 8:12; 12:46).
    2.) The deeds of Christ also reveal him as the light of the
    world.
     (a.) The miracles of Christ, especially those perform-
     ed on the blind, establish the fact that as he gives
     physical light to bodies so he also give spiritual
     light to souls.
     (b.) Christ, the light, is the victor in a confrontation with
     darkness, the symbol of sin and Satan (cf. John 1:4;
     3:19; 13:30; Luke 22:53).
   b. Christ is the light who guides us to eternal life.
    1.) The opposition between light and darkness is not
    merely a literary description of the mystery of good
    and evil—that opposition is a very real moral issue.
    2.) Individuals must make a decision in favor of the light.
     (a.) Christ, the light of men, reveals to us the know-
     ledge of God and the mystery of divine justice and
     mercy.
     (b.) It is the responsibility of each one of us to choose
     to be a "Son of Light" (cf. Luke 16:8); we must
     make the effort.
      (i.) Only the man who decides against the light
      will choose to live in darkness (cf. John 3:19).
      (ii.) One must make the effort to keep faith in

Christ; "While you have the light, keep faith in the light; thus you will become sons of light" (John 12:36).

B. Christ is our salvation in whom we place our faith.

    1. Christ reveals himself to all as their savior.

        a. The miracles performed by Christ indicate that his role is to save souls.

            1.) Our Lord performed miracles, curing the sick, saving Peter and the other Apostles from a storm at sea, and raising the dead to life.

            2.) These miracles are the outward signs of the power of Christ to save men's souls.

        b. Christ declares that the purpose of his life is to save souls.

            1.) During his life on earth Christ tells Zacchaeus and the woman afflicted with a hemorrhage that he has come to save the lost.

            2.) Our Lord's dying declaration to a repentant thief is a word of forgiveness and salvation.

    2. It is necessary to express our faith in Christ's saving action by our patience.

        a. Faith in the saving power of Christ is necessary, for Christ declares it is this faith in him that is the saving work of God (cf. John 6:28,29).

        b. Faith in the saving action of Christ is expressed by our patience.

            1.) Christ declares that it is in patience that one possesses one's soul.

            2.) We must follow the example of Christ, who being patient in his suffering, entered into his glory (cf. Phil. 3:10; Rom. 8:17).

            3.) Faith, inspiring patience, leads a soul to a tolerance of others (cf. Math. 5:45) and is an expression of our brotherly love (cf. I Cor. 13:4).

Conclusion: "The Lord is my light and my salvation; . . . have pity on me, and answer me. . . Wait for the Lord. . . " (Ps. 27:1,7,14).

MONDAY OF THE FOURTH WEEK OF LENT

Introduction: While the verses of Psalm 30* are not in chronolog-
ical order, they are nevertheless a brief biography of the psalmist.
The sacred poet gives us insights into his thinking as he mentions his
illness and recovery.

Psalm 30, the Responsorial Psalm for today's Mass, is the very
personal prayer of a sensitive soul. The psalmist expresses his
gratitude to God for the gift of health.

I The psalmist expressed his gratitude for his recovery from a near-
fatal illness.
   A. The psalmist recovered from a near-fatal illness.
      1. The psalmist did not describe his illness, but the tone of his
      account indicates that it was grave and that he had been in
      serious danger of death.
         a. During his illness the psalmist thought God was hiding
         from him.
            1.) "O Lord. . . when you hid your face I was terrified"
            (Ps. 30:8).
            2.) In his trouble the psalmist thought he had lost God's
            favor.
         b. In his serious physical condition the psalmist was
         awakened to the seriousness of his spiritual condition.
            1.) During his illness the psalmist had time to reflect.
              (a.) Before his illness the psalmist had been filled with
              self-confidence (cf. Ps. 30:7).
              (b.) The psalmist became aware that God had permit-
              ted the illness to teach him a lesson of humility.
            2.) Terrified by his physical and spiritual condition, the
            palmist cried out to God to help him (cf. Ps. 30:8-9).
      2. Using impressive figures of speech, the psalmist described
      how God had rescued him.
         a. To express his rescue by God the psalmist used a word in
         Hebrew that signified "drawing water from a deep well."
            1.) The psalmist had descended deep into misery.
              (a.) Being seriously ill was like being in a pit; the

---

*It has been suggested by some commentators that the verses of Psalm 30 should be
read in the following sequence: 6-7; 8-10; 1-3; 11-12; 4-5.

psalmist was on his way to the grave with other dying people (cf. Ps. 30:4).

    (b.) The psalmist was in the nether world as he reflected on his condition (cf. Ps. 30:4).

2.) God drew up the psalmist—rescued him (Ps. 30:4).

    (a.) God answered the prayer offered by the psalmist.

    (b.) God healed the psalmist.

b. The psalmist compared himself in his illness to a traveler arriving at an inn late in the evening (cf. Ps. 30:6).

1.) The traveler was weeping as he arrived at the inn.

    (a.) The physical discomforts of the traveler's journey included cold, hunger, thirst, and the pangs of loneliness.

    (b.) Inside the inn the traveler was warmed by a fire and the hospitality of the innkeeper.

        (i.) A good meal and a little wine refreshed the ill and exhausted traveler.

        (ii.) The companionship of his host and fellow guests comforted the traveler.

    (c.) Rested and refreshed, the traveler rejoiced as he left the inn the next morning.

2.) In his illness the psalmist was wearied to tears.

    (a.) The psalmist suffered physical pain and the pangs of loneliness, "No one cares about me."

    (b.) The psalmist found shelter in God.

        (i.) God revived his spirit.

        (ii.) The psalmist lived; he rejoiced as he thanked God who had rescued him.

B. The psalmist expressed gratitude to God for the lesson his illness had taught him.

1. In his illness the psalmist remembered a lesson he had once been taught but had forgotten.

a. In the days of his well-being the psalmist had forgotten the lesson of his dependence upon God.

b. In his suffering the psalmist remembered this lesson.

1.) Human help could not cure his illness.

2.) It was God who returned the psalmist to good health and a pleasant life.

    (a.) God was the faithful helper who alone answered the psalmist's plea for assistance.

    (b.) As the sun at dawn brightens the sky, so the pres-

ence of God and his divine help rejoiced the heart
of the psalmist (cf. Ps. 30:6).

   (i.) God changed the psalmist's mourning into
   dancing (cf. Ps. 30:12).

   (ii.) God exchanged the sackcloth of pain for the
   gladness of good health (cf. Ps. 30:12).

2. The soul of the psalmist was filled with gratitude to God.

   a. The psalmist thanked God for the spiritual lesson taught
   by his illness.

      1.) In his sorrow, which was brief, the psalmist learned a
      lifelong lesson (cf. Ps. 30:6).

      2.) The psalmist was frightened because his security rested
      on God.

   b. The psalmist was grateful for his physical recovery.

      1.) He thanked God for his recovery: "O Lord, my God,
      forever will I give you thanks" (Ps. 30:13).

      2.) The gratitude of the psalmist overflowed from his soul,
      and he invited others to join him in the hymn of thanks-
      giving: "Sing praise to the Lord, you his faithful ones,
      and give thanks to his holy name" (Ps. 30:5).

II Responding to grace, we offer the Eucharist to God in a spirit of
gratitude.

   A. We respond to the grace of God.

      1. We have to be candid as we face the needs of life.

         a. We have to be willing to gain spiritually from the mo-
         ments of distress we experience.

            1.) "God is love."

            2.) To attract our attention God permits us to suffer.

            3.) Having gained our attention, God shows us his love
            and mercy.

         b. God permits us to recover not only physically but also
         morally.

            1.) God allows us to return to life.

            2.) We are not to live as we did in the past.

      2. God's grace, our recovery, is a new chance.

         a. God answers our prayers and grants us the grace to re-
         cover from a physical illness or a moral defect.

            1.) This is a new chance given us by God.

            2.) Returning to familiar things, we are not to live in the
            familiar old way.

    b. Taking advantage of this new chance, we advance spiritually.

        1.) We pray more fervently.

        2.) We are very prompt and exact in fulfilling the duties of our vocation.

B. We express our gratitude to God in the Eucharist.

    1. We have a new way to thank God.

        a. The word "Eucharist" is first used in the New Testament.

            1.) This word "Eucharist" is a new word added to the religious vocabulary of men.

            2.) The word "Eucharist" was not known to the Hebrews.

            3.) The word "Eucharist" is used to signify "thanksgiving" after the death and resurrection of Christ.

        b. The sacrament of the Holy Eucharist is the thanksgiving we offer God.

    2. We unite ourselves with Christ present in the Holy Eucharist.

        a. At Mass we unite ourselves with Christ.

            1.) Christ dedicated himself to the Father in order that each one of us might be sanctified.

                (a.) We are in the habit of uniting ourselves with Christ in a spirit of contrition as he atones for our sins.

                (b.) We are in the habit of uniting ourselves with Christ, sacrificing himself, that we may obtain graces for our lives.

            2.) We should form the habit of uniting ourselves with the sacrifice of Christ in a spirit of gratitude.

                (a.) The sacrifice of Christ was offered to God in a spirit of gratitude.

                (b.) We can unite ourselves with Christ in the sacrifice of the Mass so that we may unite our gratitude with his and offer it to God the Father.

        b. Receiving Holy Communion, we offer our gratitude to God.

            1.) Again, as we return to our places, we unite our sentiments of gratitude with the gratitude of Christ who accepts our thanksgiving and continues to present it to the heavenly Father.

            2.) At Holy Communion we become very conscious of God's gifts and we are grateful.

                (a.) We are conscious of God's gifts—church,

kingdom of God, redemption, prayer—and each
one knows the very intimate graces he or she has
received from God.

(b.) We promise to continue our gratitude to God all
through our lives.

Conclusion: Each one of us makes the prayer of the psalmist our
lifelong sentiment: "I will extol you, O Lord, for you drew me clear.
. . I cried out to you and you healed me. . . O Lord, my God, forever
will I give you thanks. . . sing praise to the Lord, you his faithful
ones, and give thanks to his holy name" (Ps. 30:1, 3, 13, 5).

TUESDAY OF THE FOURTH WEEK OF LENT

Introduction: The same theme runs through Psalms 46, 47, and 48.
The individual who wrote these psalms was inspired by a historical
event. During the reign of Hezekiah, the nation was in danger of
invasion by the army of Sennacherib, but through the mercy of God
the danger was averted.

The Responsorial Psalm for today's Mass, Psalm 46, is a prayer of
confidence in God. It invites believers and nonbelievers alike:
"Come, behold the deeds of the Lord" (Ps. 46:9).

I Unshakable confidence in God brings joy to the soul of a devout
Israelite.

  A. Devout Israelites placed their confidence in God.

    1. In times of danger devout Israelites placed their confidence
in God.

      a. The Israelites knew the possibility of great danger.

        1.) There was the danger of an invasion: "Though nations
are in turmoil, kingdoms totter . . ." (Ps. 46:7).

        2.) There was a possibility of the destruction of the earth:
". . .though the earth be shaken and mountains plunge
into the sea; though its waters rage and foam and the
mountains quake at its surging" (Ps. 46:3-4).

      b. The Israelites were called to place their confidence in
God.

        1.) Some Israelites wanted to enlist the aid of Egypt to
repel the invading army.

        2.) The Israelites were urged to consider that, just as God

controlled nature and protected the nation from such natural disasters as earthquakes and floods, so God alone could protect their country from invasion.

(a.) The Israelites knew of God's power over nature; trusting God, the people would learn of his power over their enemies.

(b.) "God is our refuge and our strength, an ever present help in distress" (Ps. 46:1).

2. Events justified the devout Israelites who trusted God.

a. Through God's help the invading army was repulsed.

1.) Just as God was the protection of the Israelites in times of natural upheavals, so he protected them from political turmoil and military disaster.

2.) God was the defense of his people.

(a.) The victory over the Assyrian army was an "astounding event" (cf. Ps. 46:9).

(b.) This victory was due to God who stopped the war, broke the bow, splintered the spear, and burned the shields (cf. Ps. 46:10).

b. God's protection of the Israelites was a sign of his presence among them.

1.) There was no human power that could destroy the People of God.

(a.) "God is our refuge and our strength, an ever present help in distress" (Ps. 46:1).

(b.) ". . . The Lord of hosts is with us" (Ps. 46:4).

2.) These verses imply that because God had chosen to dwell in Israel he would not permit it to be destroyed.

B. The devout Israelite could rejoice in God.

1. The psalmist used the poetic image of a flowing river to express his thoughts of God.

a. "There is a stream whose runlets gladden the city of God" (Ps. 46:5).

1.) A stream flows gently, quietly; an Israelite sitting on its bank enjoyed the peace and security of his surroundings.

2.) God was present to Israel, and he was gentle to those who trusted him to give them peace and security.

b. A stream running through the land enriches the soil; similarly God enriched Israel.

1.) Israel could enjoy the fruits of the harvest that were the products of God's goodness.

    2.) Spiritually Israel was enriched by God who let the people know he was present to them and concerned with their well-being.

2. Israel was invited to persevere in its joy.

    a. "Come, behold the deeds of the Lord, the astounding things he has wrought on earth" (Ps. 46:9).

    b. Israel could be joyful if it remembered all that God had done for the nation.

        1.) Israel was to reflect on the goodness of God toward the nation.

        2.) Israel would be a joy-filled nation as long as its people remembered what had happened.

            (a.) Remembered once, this would prompt Israel to place its trust in God.

            (b.) If they failed to remember God's goodness, if they failed to trust him, they would be destroyed.

II We place our confidence in God and find joy.

    A. We place our confidence in God.

        1. We face the reality that we experience many fears.

            a. We know the physical fear caused by sickness or by such forces of nature as floods, hurricanes, and earthquakes.

            b. We know at times a psychological fear caused by insecurity and loneliness.

            c. We accept the fact that we are afraid, and we try to cope with our fears.

                1.) In this effort some of us have tried patent medicines, alcohol, and psychogenics; perhaps we have either denied or laughed at our fears, dreamed of Utopia, or danced at Camelot.

                    (a.) The fears have not disappeared.

                    (b.) The problems still demand a solution, and questions must be answered.

                2.) To cope with our fears we must accept certain truths.

                    (a.) Perhaps the most difficult truth to accept is that of our own limitations.

                    (b.) We must be willing to work with these limitations and contribute to the well-being of our neighbors.

        2. In all circumstances of life we trust God.

            a. God is the one Reality we must find in all our experiences.

1.) In moments of loneliness God is the refuge who offers us shelter in trouble, the company of his presence, and the security of his support.

2.) In moments of insecurity God offers us his strength and his help.

  b. Our security is trust in God's wisdom and power.

    1.) God in his wisdom permits all the events of our life.

      (a.) God has a purpose that governs all the events of our life.

      (b.) Confidence is our willingness to choose the wisdom of God in preference to our limited knowledge.

      (c.) Confidence is reliance upon God's power.

    2.) Our confidence in God is tested when we suffer.

      (a.) Our faith strengthens our confidence as we realize that the power of God brings good out of every evil.

      (b.) By the power of God, evil contributes to God's glory in a very mysterious way.

B. We find joy in God by reflecting on his goodness.

  1. God is the source of our joy.

    a. God is present; we are always before him.

      1.) There is no place where we can go and fail to find God.

      2.) Nothing that touches our lives escapes the attention of God.

    b. We know that the presence of God is our joy.

      1.) God comes to us when we pray.

      2.) God forgives our sins.

      3.) God allows us to fulfill his purpose.

        (a.) God calls us to share the joy of the resurrection of Christ by participating in the pain and sorrow of Christ's passion and death.

        (b.) The trials and fears of this life will come to an end, but our joy will last forever.

  2. We reflect on these truths.

    a. In our moments of reflection tensions are eased.

      1.) We take the time to think, to reflect with faith on our lives.

        (a.) We step back from the fear and tension and examine our situation with the supernatural light of faith.

(b.) We think of God's presence in our life.
2.) We are interested in knowing God.
(a.) We find the divine Will in our daily experiences.
(b.) We relate our experiences to the life of Christ.
b. We recall God's goodness to us.
1.) We consider how often God has shown us his power by the assistance he offers us.
2.) We consider the mercy of God, recalling that he sent his Son to redeem us and that God forgives our sins.

Conclusion: We accept the ancient invitation of the psalmist: "Come, behold the deeds of the Lord, the astounding things he has wrought on earth" (Ps. 46:9). "Therefore we fear not . . ." (Ps. 46:3). God is in our midst; we shall not be disturbed; God will help (cf. Ps. 46:3, 5-6).

WEDNESDAY OF THE FOURTH WEEK OF LENT

Introduction: The Responsorial Psalm for today's Mass, Psalm 145, is the first of the group of psalms that conclude the Psalter. The verses of these psalms have served to inspire many prayers of benediction and thanksgiving. For centuries Psalm 145 has been an essential part of the daily prayers of the Jewish people. It also has an honored place in Christian worship.

Psalm 145 praises God for his fidelity and mercy. Looking at the universe with the eyes of the psalmist, one wonders if today we could combine our scientific knowledge of the universe with the prayer of the psalmist and join in his praise of God.

I The psalmist declared that God was to be praised for his fidelity and mercy.
  A. The psalmist declared that God was to be praised.
    1. "I will extol you, O my God and King, and I will bless your name forever and ever" (Ps. 145:1).
      a. In his psalm the writer repeated this thought several times.
      b. God, the King of the universe, was different from all other kings.
        1.) God was good to all creatures without exception.
        2.) God provided for all his creatures and was a savior for all people.

2. The psalmist did not take the time to prove the greatness of the kingship of God.

    a. The psalmist thought the universe made the greatness of God's kingship self-evident (cf. Ps. 145:12).

    b. The psalmist stated that God was a benevolent king and therefore all generations would praise him (cf. Ps. 145:4).

B. God was to be praised because he had shown fidelity and mercy to Israel.

  1. God was faithful to Israel.

    a. God was unchangeable, true to his word which does not pass away.

      1.) God made the universe, and by his word he ruled the world.

      2.) In the sense that God provided for his creatures he was faithful to them.

    b. God kept all his promises to Israel.

      1.) God kept his promise to liberate Israel from her enemies.

      2.) Faithful to his promise, God bound Israel to himself in the Covenant.

  2. God was merciful to Israel.

    a. For the Israelites the mercy of God was not automatically associated with his goodness.

    b. To the Hebrew mind God was conscious of his goodness, and he freely willed to show his compassion and freely willed to pardon sin.

      1.) God showed his mercy by his compassion for the poor and by his protection of those who prayed to him.

      2.) The mercy of God was shown by his freedom in granting pardon to the Israelites.

        (a.) God willed the salvation of the Israelites and freely pardoned those who offended him.

        (b.) God is merciful, giving support to the weakness of human nature.

      3.) The great manifestation of God's mercy was his freedom to enact the Covenant with Israel.

II Today we can use our knowledge of the universe to praise God.

  A. The modern investigation of the universe reveals the fidelity and mercy of God.

    1. Today we study our planet.

    a. Through scientific investigation we study the sky, the earth, and the sea.

    b. We learn of God's fidelity and mercy.

      1.) God does not change the laws of nature.

      2.) God has allowed scientific investigation to bring about the enrichment of human life.

2. Today we explore space.

    a. We have been able to study the heavenly bodies by telescope, by probes, and by a landing on Mars.

    b. This has made known to us God's fidelity and mercy.

      1.) These explorations have increased our knowledge of God's creation.

      2.) These studies have given us an insight into man's role in the universe.

3. Today human nature is an object of study and investigation.

    a. As we advance the knowledge of the physical life of man, we know God has been faithful to the laws he established governing human growth and development.

    b. The study of human emotions and passions reveals the mercy of God, who grants his grace and help so that we may cope with life.

B. The modern investigation of creation leads us to praise God.

1. We can say that we ". . . discourse of the glory of your kingdom and speak of your might . . . making known to men your might and the glorious splendor of your kingdom" (Ps. 145:11-12).

    a. As we discuss the nature of various cell structures, the laws of energy, and the like, we must think and talk of the power of God who created the universe.

      1.) We must think of the divine power, which controls the energy of the universe by a word.

      2.) We shall be that generation which praises the work of God and proclaims his might (cf. Ps. 145:4).

    b. We praise God: "Your kingdom is a kingdom for all ages, and your dominion endures through all generations" (Ps. 145:13).

      1.) The vast sky, the deep sea, and the constantly spinning planets are a reflection of the eternity of God.

      2.) As we study hurricanes, earthquakes, and floods, we are reminded of the power of God.

        (a.) These acts of nature are "making known to men

your might . . ." (Ps. 145:12).

- (b.) Even in the destruction caused by storms and floods we have evidence of God's power and goodness.
    - (i.) The experience of natural upheavals shows the power of God bringing good out of evil.
    - (ii.) These experiences direct our attention to the need for prayer, and we learn that "the Lord is near to all who call upon him . . ." (Ps. 145: 18).

2. The modern study of human nature leads us to praise the mercy of God.
    - a. When we study human behavior, we must realize that "the Lord lifts up all who are falling and raises up all who are bowed down" (Ps. 145:14).
    - b. The knowledge of human emotions reveals to us that "the Lord is gracious and merciful, slow to anger and of great kindness" (Ps. 145:8).
    - c. We consider the human effort to improve life, and we say to God: "The eyes of all look hopefully to you, and you give them their food in due season; you open your hand and satisfy the desire of every living thing" (Ps. 145:15-16).

Conclusion: Our present concern with science does not divert our attention from God. It focuses our minds on the fact that "the Lord is just in all his ways and holy in all his works" (Ps. 145:17). There-fore each one prays: "May my mouth speak the praise of the Lord, and may all flesh bless his holy name forever and ever" (Ps. 145:21).

THURSDAY OF THE FOURTH WEEK OF LENT

Introduction: The theme of national infidelity that runs through to-day's Responsorial Psalm may not be so strange to us as it was to previous generations. Psalm 106, however, does not use this theme as a political weapon, deadly to one's opponents, nor does it con-sider national dishonor a platform from which to declare self-righteousness.

Psalm 106 is a national lament that cries out for the spiritual re-newal of Israel. Spiritual renewal is a theme that we can consider.

I History taught the Israelites that God gave them a mediator.

  A. The psalmist reminded Israel of its history.

    1. The psalmist recorded the history of Israel to show that the well-being of the nation depended upon its obedience to the Will of God.

      a. In the first part of Psalm 106 the psalmist reviewed the history of Israel to show that God was true to his word.

      b. The second part of Psalm 106 is a record of Israel's forgetfulness of God's mercy and of the consequences of that forgetfulness.

    2. Certain historical facts were recorded in Psalm 106 for the purpose of reminding Israel of God's mercy.

      a. The fact that Israel was disloyal to God could not be denied.

        1.) The failures of Israel were not recorded to shame the nation.

        2.) The psalmist wanted the nation to face the reality of its sin.

          (a.) If Israel remembered its history, the nation would remain faithful to God.

          (b.) In its sin of infidelity Israel could find hope for its salvation.

      b. The mercy of God emerges from the history of Israel more than does the sin of the Israelites.

        1.) The history of Israel was the record of God's mercy.

          (a.) God watched over the people he had chosen as his own.

          (b.) God was ever mindful of his Covenant with Israel.

        2.) God in his mercy raised up Moses as the defender of the Israelites (cf. Ps. 106:23).

  B. Moses was the mediator between the Israelites and God.

    1. "Then he spoke of exterminating them, but Moses, his chosen one, withstood him in the breach to turn back his destructive wrath" (Ps. 106:23).

      a. The impression of this verse is that of a military action in which a soldier with raw courage stands alone, risking his life to defend his country.

      b. No doubt Moses acted with great courage, but he was the chosen one of God.

        1.) Moses acted under the inspiration of God's goodness and not by his own personal whim.

2.) Moses acted and succeeded because a merciful God willed it.
2. Moses was a true mediator for the Israelites.
    a. Moses was given the task of leading the Israelites to the Promised Land.
        1.) Moses was directed by the divine wisdom as he lead the Israelites from Egypt and through the trials of the desert journey, during which he suffered from the envy of others (cf. Ps. 106:6).
        2.) In God's name Moses spoke to the Israelites, directing them on their journey and educating them in the meaning of the Covenant.
    b. Moses was appointed by God as the intercessor for the Israelites.
        1.) It was through the prayers of Moses that God granted victory to Israel.
        2.) God mercifully answered the prayers of Moses, pardoning the sins of Israel and saving the nation from death.
        3.) In response to his selection by God, Moses acted as leader, legislator, and mediator for the Israelites.

II We live in our need for a mediator, Christ.
  A. We live in our need.
    1. We must admit that sin is the cause of our greatest need.
      a. We cannot escape the reality of sin or be indifferent to it.
        1.) We cannot escape the reality of sin because we experience it in our lives.
          (a.) The easy explanations offered for human failure are no longer accepted.
          (b.) We are beginning to realize that the greatest sin is to say, "There is no sin."
            (i.) Such remarks reveal a heart that is insincere and proud.
            (ii.) We are now beginning to realize that sin is not only possible but that it is the cause of much human distress.
        2.) Once again indifference to sin is becoming unpopular.
          (a.) The excuses of a few years ago, "Man is like that" or "Well, what are you going to do?" are no longer acceptable.

        (b.) A swelling tide of public opinion demands a confession of sin.

    b. We believe that sin is the cause of our greatest need.

        1.) Many of the promising experiments for human improvement have not relieved human misery and suffering.

        2.) We hear the loud cry for change.

  2. We admit our need for spiritual change.

    a. We remember our history.

        1.) We admit that our hopes have been destroyed and our plans for improvement frustrated.

        2.) Our history teaches us the need for spiritual renewal.

           (a.) This Lent we have generously performed acts of personal repentance.

           (b.) To achieve this spiritual renewal, we have experienced many personal struggles and even frustration.

    b. A spiritual change is possible.

        1.) We do not despair because we see the light of hope and joy.

        2.) "God so loved the world that he gave his only Son, that whoever believes in him may not die but may have eternal life" (John 3:16).

B. We live in dependence on Christ.

  1. Christ has been sent by the Father to be the guide of the New People of God.

    a. To be a guide for others one must have a knowledge of the terrain over which the journey is to be made.

        1.) This knowledge is required because without it one cannot show another the route of the journey.

        2.) The people making a journey trust the guide, and he deceives them if he does not know the way.

    b. We can depend on Christ for guidance on our journey to heaven.

        1.) "No one has gone up to heaven except the One who came down from there—the Son of Man . . ." (John 3:13).

        2.) We "have faith in the One whom he sent" (John 6:29).

           (a.) We live trusting Christ.

           (b.) Our Lord has been where we are going, and he is there still.

2. Christ is our intercessor before God the Father.
  a. Our Lord took upon himself our humanity, and he offered himself for us.
    1.) Through his death and resurrection we have the hope of a better life.
    2.) Our Lord obtained grace for us and pardon for our sins, and through him we have the hope of eternal life.
  b. Our Lord's prayers are always heard.
    1.) On earth Our Lord prayed for us, and the Father answered his prayers.
    2.) Now in the glory of heaven Christ continues to make intercession for us.
      (a.) The Father answers the prayers of Christ; the Father grants us his pardon and mercy.
      (b.) We depend on the prayers of Christ for our change of heart, our spiritual renewal.

Conclusion: History is not merely a record of human failure, misery, and sin. History is the record of God's mercy, and we "Give thanks to the Lord, for he is good, for his kindness endures forever" (Ps. 106:1).

FRIDAY OF THE FOURTH WEEK OF LENT

Introduction: In the Responsorial Psalm for today's Mass the psalmist expressed his gratitude for the fear of God. To our present way of thinking this is strange.

In the popular mind the religion of the Old Testament appears as one of fear. It seems to us that the Old Testament religion was without love, joy, or laughter. We also think that God was stern and forbidding to the people of the Old Testament and quick to punish them. We picture life of the Old Testament as very limited in its good times and always under the cloud of gloom. It was depressing, we say. We wonder why the psalmist was grateful for such a way of life. However we have to admit that the popular idea of Old Testament religion is not correct. The law of love governed the law of fear, and it is that for which the psalmist was grateful.

I The psalmist was grateful for the security he found in the fear of God.

A. The psalmist had a religious fear of God.
1. The psalmist was not speaking of a human fear.
   a. The psalmist did not stand before God as one would stand before a menacing enemy.
   b. The fear of God did not make the psalmist wince under the lash of a taskmaster.
2. The fear of God experienced by the psalmist was rooted in the love of God.
   a. To the psalmist the fear of God was a personal religious experience.
      1.) The psalmist feared God because he loved God and respected him.
      2.) The psalmist had experienced God's love.
         (a.) The psalmist knew that God saw and heard those who were in need and that he answered their prayers.
         (b.) The psalmist had been among the "brokenhearted," those "crushed in spirit," and those who were in the greatest need (cf. Ps. 34:19).
   b. God came to aid the psalmist; in turn the psalmist loved God.
      1.) God came to the aid of the psalmist.
         (a.) God rescued the psalmist from his enemies.
         (b.) God helped the psalmist in his time of trial.
      2.) In turn the psalmist loved God.
         (a.) The love of the psalmist for God was manifested by the respect the psalmist had for him.
         (b.) The psalmist tried to do God's Will.
B. The psalmist was grateful for the security he found in God.
1. The psalmist experienced security in the fear of God.
   a. The psalmist found security in God.
      1.) The psalmist directed his life toward God.
      2.) The psalmist was aware that what God directed was good and that what he willed made life enjoyable, provided one obeyed the divine will.
   b. The security he found in God did not free the psalmist from suffering.
      1.) Experience taught the psalmist that his security and love for God did not excuse him from suffering.
         (a.) The psalmist knew that a religious soul could be victimized in many ways.

(b.) Having experienced suffering, the psalmist knew
he was protected by God (cf. Ps. 34:20).

2.) In his suffering the psalmist realized the deep spiritual
realities of life.

(a.) From his experience the psalmist knew that one
who remained close to God might be hurt but
would never be permanently disabled (cf. Ps.
34:21).

(b.) However the wicked, those who stray from God,
do not recover and "they pay for their guilt" (cf.
Ps. 34:22).

2. The psalmist was grateful.

a. The psalmist realized his sufferings were not intended by
God to be frightening.

1.) God intended to reassure the psalmist by this suffering.

2.) ". . . the Lord redeems the lives of his servants; no one
incurs guilt who takes refuge in him" (Ps. 34:23).

b. The psalmist was grateful for the love God had given him.

1.) The psalmist realized that God was his Father.

2.) The psalmist was thankful for the lesson he had
learned: A long and prosperous life was possible because God loved him.

II We are grateful for the gift of Fear of the Lord.

A. We possess the gift of Fear of the Lord.

1. The gift of Fear of the Lord was given to us at baptism.

a. In the sacrament of baptism we were adopted by God as
his children.

b. The gift of Fear of the Lord enables us to live as children
of God.

1.) The gift of Fear of the Lord inspires us to approach
God as our Father.

2.) The gift of Fear of the Lord prompts us to show God
respect.

(a.) The Fear of the Lord increases our desire to be
united with God as a child is united with his father.

(b.) The Fear of the Lord directs us to obey the Will of
God.

2. The gift of Fear of the Lord gives us the reassurance we need
in life.

  a. Christ frequently greeted his Apostles with the salutation, "Fear not."

    1.) The Apostles were not meant to live in a state of human fear.

      (a.) When the storm arose on the sea during the hours of three and six in the morning, Christ reassured the Apostles (cf. Mark 6:47-51).

      (b.) In times of physical suffering the Apostles were not to be afraid but were to depend on God (cf. Matt. 10:28).

    2.) The Apostles were not to worry about their status.

      (a.) The Father had given the Apostles the kingdom of heaven (cf. Luke 12:32).

      (b.) The Apostles, as they governed the Church, were not to be afraid but were to have peace of mind (cf. John 20:21 ff.).

  b. Our Lord gives us reassurance.

    1.) Through the gift of Fear of the Lord we know that God protects us during the storms of life.

    2.) Christ is our brother, and through the gift of Fear of the Lord we are united with him as children of God.

      (a.) For the welfare of the Church we unite our physical and mental sufferings to the suffering of Christ.

      (b.) The Fear of the Lord assures us that we are those to whom God gives the kingdom of heaven.

      (c.) The Fear of the Lord assures us that our sins are forgiven by a loving Father.

B. We express our gratitude to God for the gift of the Fear of the Lord.

  1. Through this gift God bestows on us a great dignity.

    a. We live in the assurance that we are children of God.

    b. This is our dignity.

  2. We express our gratitude to God.

    a. In our daily prayers we thank God, using our own words and speaking to God as a child talks to his father.

    b. Our lives are an expression of our gratitude.

      1.) We accept the Will of God in all the events of life.

      2.) We place our confidence in God as a child trusts his father, knowing God protects us.

Conclusion: We have learned the lesson of the Fear of God that "...

nought is lacking to those who fear him . . . those who seek the Lord want for no good thing" (Ps. 34:10, 11). We "bless the Lord at all times . . ." (Ps. 34:1).

SATURDAY OF THE FOURTH WEEK OF LENT

Introduction: The Responsorial Psalm for today's Mass, Psalm 7, is a prayer of confidence. Probably it was composed by David while he was being pursued by Saul.

The psalmist, unjustly accused by his enemies, declared his innocence, and he had no doubt that he would be delivered from his enemies. He prayed with confidence in God.

I In a time of danger the psalmist expressed his confidence in God.
   A. The psalmist was in danger.
      1. The psalmist was attacked by many under the direction of Saul.
      2. The psalmist used a vivid image to express his danger.
         a. "Lest I become like the lion's prey, to be torn to pieces, with no one to rescue" (Ps. 7:3).
            1.) The psalmist compared his enemies' attack on him to the attack of a lion.
            2.) The anger of the psalmist's enemies was like the rage of a lion.
         b. Both the attack of the lion and the rage of the psalmist's enemies were without reason.
   B. The psalmist placed his trust in God.
      1. The psalmist pleaded with God for help and deliverance.
         a. The psalmist did not place his trust in human help.
            1.) There were political reasons for such caution.
               (a.) Saul, the psalmist's foe, had many agents.
               (b.) David could have been betrayed by anyone in return for a favor from Saul.
            2.) The psalmist was very much aware of the limitations of human assistance, which could not free him from attack.
         b. The psalmist prayed with confidence to God.
      2. The psalmist used an impressive image to express his confidence in God.
         a. He compared God to a judge who has convened his court.

(cf. Ps. 7:7-9).
  1.) The psalmist, the innocent party in the suit, appealed
      with confidence to the judge (cf. Ps. 7:9).
      (a.) The psalmist was confident that his innocence
           would be established.
      (b.) David had no evil intentions; he had spared Saul's
           life: "I who spared those who without cause were
           my foes" (Ps. 7:5).
  2.) David's enemies, the wicked, would be exposed in
      their malice.
      (a.) The psalmist's enemies would not be able to com-
           plete their plans to destroy him.
      (b.) The psalmist's enemies would be declared guilty.
  b. The psalmist rested his defense on the justice of God.
     1.) God was just and he protected the innocent.
     2.) Every day God was indignant with the wicked (cf. Ps.
         7:12).

II We place a joyful trust in God.
  A. We must admit that evil does exist and that with God's help we
       can conquer it.
       1. While we admit the existence of evil, we acknowledge the
          power and mercy of God.
          a. We admit the presence of evil.
             1.) Moral corruption is on all sides, together with much
                 that deprives us of happiness.
             2.) We admit that we are sinners.
          b. We acknowledge the power and mercy of God.
             1.) God is merciful, wishing us to grow in holiness: "It is
                 God's will that you grow in holiness . . ." (I Thess. 4:3).
             2.) God is powerful; he has lifted us from the depths of sin
                 to the dignity of a child of God.
       2. We place our confidence in God's help.
          a. Our Lord directed us to be like children: "I assure you that
             whoever does not accept the reign of God like a little
             child shall not take part in it" (Mark 10:15).
             1.) When a child requests anything of his father, the
                 youngster is confident his father will provide it.
             2.) Our Lord told us to have a childlike confidence in
                 God our Father (cf. Luke 11:9-13).
          b. We repeat in our lives the experience of Christ.

1.) We may be mocked as Christ was, and like him we may have to suffer many things.

2.) We follow the example of Christ who in the agony of death was confident of his Father's help: "Father, into your hands I commend my spirit" (Luke 23:46).

B. Our confidence is a joyful trust in God.

1. We do not depend upon ourselves.

a. We know our limitations.

b. We know that we stand in great need.

2. We rest on God's reliability.

a. Like Christ we are determined to do the Will of our heavenly Father.

1.) We follow Christ that in him we may find joy and peace (cf. John 16:33).

2.) We are certain that living this way we "lack no spiritual gift" as we "wait for the revelation of our Lord Jesus Christ" (I Cor. 1:7).

(a.) There is nothing that can separate us from God (cf. Rom. 8:38).

(b.) There is nothing that can destroy us; rather every experience, good or bad, only serves to improve our lives, for "we know that God makes all things work together for the good of those who have been called according to his decree" (Rom. 8:28).

b. We are filled with joy because of God who helps us.

1.) Like Christ we remain faithful ". . . as the Son placed over God's house. It is we who are that house if we hold fast to our confidence and the hope of which we boast" (Heb. 3:6).

2.) We are not alone: "For we do not have a high priest who is unable to sympathize with our weakness, but one who was tempted in every way that we are, yet never sinned. So let us confidently approach the throne of grace to receive mercy and favor and to find help in the time of need" (Heb. 4:15-16).

3.) This union with God, our dependence upon him, is our joy—a promise of our eternal joy.

Conclusion: "O Lord, my God, in you I take refuge . . ." (Ps. 7:1). We know that "he who has begun the good work in you will carry it through to completion, right up to the day of Christ Jesus" (Phil. 1:6).

THE FIFTH SUNDAY OF LENT

Introduction: The first reading of today's Mass is a message of hope. As the prophet Isaiah offered the hope of a new Exodus to the Israelites during their exile, so the Church offers us the hope of the resurrection, our Exodus, during our exile on earth.

Like the Israelites in exile we may be discouraged. But today we can see that the purpose of our lives, and in particular of our Lenten works, is to participate in the resurrection of Christ.

I The Israelites were reminded that they were the Chosen People of God.
   A. God reminded Israel that he had called them his own people.
      1. The first reading of today's Mass from the prophet Isaiah reminded Israel of its vocation.
         a. Inspired by God, the prophet spoke to the Israelites during a time of national disgrace.
            1.) Many times God had shown Israel his love and mercy.
            2.) As a nation Israel had rejected God's love and mercy.
               (a.) The consequences of this rejection of divine love were extensive.
               (b.) Many Israelites were put to death by an invading army; the nation was conquered and those who survived were led into exile.
         b. The nation needed a reminder of its vocation.
            1.) The Israelites, like any displaced people or prisoners of war, were desperate.
            2.) The Israelites needed the reassurance that they were chosen by God as his own people.
      2. Through the prophet, God told the Israelites to make use of their past history as a lesson for their present condition.
         a. "Remember not the events of the past, the things of long ago consider not" (Isa. 43:18).
         b. The Israelites were told by God not to glory in their past but to learn a lesson from their history.
            1.) The history of Israel was the history of salvation.
               (a.) The history of Israel was a record of economic and political changes as well as of military campaigns.

(b.) Principally, however, the history of Israel was the record of God's saving action in the life of Israel.

2.) The nation had disobeyed God and was judged by him as guilty; nonetheless God showed Israel his mercy and love.

B. Through the prophet Isaiah, God sent the Israelites the message of hope.

1. God had not forgotten the Israelites in their time of need.

a. Once again God had taken the initiative.

b. "See, I am doing something new" (Isa. 43:19).

1.) The great deeds God had done for Israel in the past would be overshadowed by this new deed God was doing.

2.) God cared for the Israelites; they were not abandoned.

2. In the suffering of the exile God was saving Israel.

a. In the exile the Israelites were like wanderers in a desert who are without water.

b. Israel had no right to expect any help.

1.) But in his mercy God gave Israel hope of being restored to its place in his affections.

2.) Using images drawn from nature, the prophet illustrated God's saving plan for the Israelites.

(a.) Abundant water was to flow in the arid desert.

(b.) The salvation of Israel was to be so extensive that the wild beasts would honor God.

3.) Israel was to be saved.

(a.) Israel would drink the water flowing in the desert: a sign of divine favor and blessings.

(b.) Israel was again "The people I formed for myself, that they might announce my praise" (Isa. 43:21).

II God is preparing us for a new Exodus.

A. During these days of Lent God is redeeming us.

1. The liturgy unfolds for us the mystery of our redemption.

a. In Mass we celebrate sacramentally the death and resurrection of Christ.

b. The readings of the Lenten Masses remind us that God promised to redeem us and that we are to cooperate with God's grace.

1.) In the Lenten readings we hear how the life of Christ led the Scribes and Pharisees to a personal crisis.

2.) These leaders of the people were to make a decision to accept or to reject Christ.

2. The liturgy is disposing us for a more intimate participation in the mystery of our redemption.

a. In the celebration of Mass we share in the death and resurrection of Christ.

b. The readings during Mass remind us that we have to make a faith-decision.

1.) We are reminded that we cannot be followers of Christ who call out to him, "Lord, Lord."

2.) We realize that the faith-decision we make demands our total dedication to Christ.

B. God is preparing us for a new journey.

1. The liturgy is leading us out of our exile.

a. As we struggle with the temptation to forget our dedication to Christ, we feel like the ancient Israelites in the desert.

1.) We feel that we are wandering without water in a trackless wasteland.

2.) We try to make a trail for ourselves so that we shall not become lost.

(a.) The storm of temptation rises and the trail is obliterated.

(b.) The storm can be so intense that we are left in darkness and see no light to guide us.

b. The liturgy offers the death and resurrection of Christ as our guide.

1.) The death and resurrection of Christ is our escape route from Satan and sin.

2.) The death and resurrection of Christ is our guidepost in the desert of temptation.

2. This is our new journey which will terminate in heaven.

a. This is a new journey for us.

1.) We have never been to heaven, but we have the certain hope that we are on the way to eternal life.

(a.) We are sure of our destination because the death and resurrection of Christ is the promise of our eternal happiness.

(b.) We are certain of the trail we follow, for it has been marked out for us by Christ.

2.) This journey is a new experience for us.

           (a.) We admit that our past efforts have failed, but we hear God say: "Remember not the events of the past, the things of long ago consider not" (Isa. 43:18).

           (b.) With renewed spiritual energy we begin the journey again, or strengthened by grace we continue the journey.

     b. God speaks to us: "See I am doing something new" (Isa. 43:19).

       1.) God is conforming us to Christ.

       2.) When the journey is over we shall be with Christ.

Conclusion: For the rest of our lives we shall be known by God as "the people whom I formed for myself, that they might announce my praise" (Isa. 43:21).

THE FIFTH SUNDAY OF LENT

Introduction: In the second reading for today's Mass St. Paul spoke of a change that took place in his life. After his experience on the road to Damascus, St. Paul had to change the values of a life that he cherished. On the Damascus road St. Paul received the grace of conversion, and three days later he was baptized (cf. Acts 9:3-19). Then he examined his life and his attitude toward Christ.

I St. Paul changed his life in the light of his faith in Christ.

  A. St. Paul said he counted all as loss (cf. Phil. 3:8).

    1. St. Paul considered his advantages as loss.

      a. St. Paul had enjoyed many advantages as a Pharisee.

        1.) Prior to his conversion St. Paul had been respected in the community of Jerusalem.

        2.) He had been known for his zeal as a champion of the Law; he had been respected for his knowledge and observance of the Law.

      b. St. Paul had to change his life and his standard of conduct.

        1.) St. Paul considered his advantages as loss for the sake of Christ.

        2.) After his conversion St. Paul saw no value in his former role in the synagogue.

    2. St. Paul's "surpassing knowledge" of Christ was the reason

for the judgment he made.

a. This "surpassing knowledge" of Christ's death and resurrection was a new experience for St. Paul.

   1.) The knowledge of Christ's death and resurrection was the foundation of Paul's holiness (justice).

      (a.) It was a new experience for St. Paul because his holiness was not founded on the exact observance of the Law.

      (b.) Faith in the death and resurrection of Christ was the basis of holiness, and on this faith St. Paul stood before God the Father.

   2.) The new experience for St. Paul was that "I have been grasped by Christ" (Phil. 3:12).

      (a.) St. Paul's new experience of faith was not only an intellectual acceptance of the death and resurrection of Christ; it also involved Paul's whole life.

      (b.) The life of St. Paul was being shaped by the death and resurrection of Christ.

b. In the light of the knowledge of Christ, St. Paul considered everything as "loss" or "rubbish" (cf. Phil. 3:8).

   1.) Through faith St. Paul was living "in Christ" (cf. Phil. 3:9).

   2.) That he might come "to know Christ and the power flowing from his resurrection; likewise to know how to share in his sufferings by being formed into the pattern of his death," St. Paul "forfeited everything" (cf. Phil. 3:10,8).

B. St. Paul's identification with Christ was not complete in the Apostle's life on earth.

   1. To illustrate his meaning St. Paul used the image of an athlete (cf. Phil. 3:12 ff.).

      a. An athlete does not look back over his shoulder to see how many others may be following him.

      b. The runner keeps his eyes to the front, looking forward that he may see the finish line and reach it to win the race.

   2. St. Paul did not concentrate on the past.

      a. He had received the gift of faith from God (cf. Phil. 3:9).

      b. Now St. Paul realized that he had to be "racing to grasp the prize" (cf. Phil. 3:12).

         1.) St. Paul made every effort to share the death of Christ.

         2.) Through faith St. Paul shared the life of the risen Christ.

3. St. Paul looked forward to the end of his life on earth.
   a. "It is not that I have reached it yet, or have already finished my course . . ." (Phil. 3:12).
   b. Like the runner in the race, St. Paul was looking forward to the finish line; there he would grasp the prize.
      1.) In the glory of heaven St. Paul would be in Christ.
      2.) There in heaven St. Paul would grasp Christ as Christ had seized him and he would have his "life on high in Christ Jesus" (cf. Phil. 3:14).

II We must live our lives with faith in the death and resurrection of Christ.
   A. We believe that Christ died and rose from the dead.
      1. Our faith in the death and resurrection of Christ involves our lives.
         a. Faith in the mystery of our redemption is more to us than an intellectual position we may take in a debate or conversation with a friend.
         b. Faith in the death and resurrection of Christ is a way of life for us.
      2. Our faith in the mystery of our redemption urges us to make changes in the way we live.
         a. This faith prompts us to conform to the death of Christ.
            1.) This demands the repudiation of the world, which is opposed to Christ.
            2.) For us such a repudiation is not a negative way of life.
               (a.) It is not a complete denial of all that is good in human living.
               (b.) It is a deliberate choice we make to die to selfishness and our passions.
         b. Faith allows the resurrection of Christ to influence our way of living.
            1.) Faith prompts us to dedicate ourselves and all that is good to the glory of God.
            2.) Faith in the resurrection of Christ is expressed by our trusting Christ so that, sharing in his death, we live in the hope of rising with him.
   B. Living in the faith of the death and resurrection of Christ is a continuous process of growth.
      1. In baptism we receive the gift of faith in the death and resurrection of Christ.

    a. In the sacrament of baptism we are conformed to the death and resurrection of Christ.

      1.) In the sacrament of baptism we conform to the death of Christ by our renouncement of Satan and sin.

      2.) In our baptism we conform to the resurrection of Christ by our dedication to God.

    b. For us the reception of the sacrament of baptism is not merely a religious rite that attracts us for a few moments.

      1.) The sacrament of baptism gives us the gift of faith in Christ's death and resurrection.

      2.) The sacrament of baptism is only the beginning of our conformation to Christ.

2. Our faith in the mystery of our redemption must grow.

    a. We have been redeemed by Christ, but we are still living in time and on earth.

      1.) We do not live in the glory of the resurrection.

        (a.) We do not possess this gift perfectly.

        (b.) Baptism has given us only the beginning of eternal life.

      2.) Each day this life must grow and develop as we use the time given to us by God for this purpose.

    b. We are constantly striving to attain the glory of the resurrection.

      1.) Like the runner of a race we keep our eyes fixed on the finish line and the prize.

        (a.) Each day we live is like a stride taken by a runner—it brings us closer to the prize, the reward of eternal glory.

        (b.) Day by day we renew the consecration of self to God, and we allow this renewal to be reflected in our daily work.

      2.) We go forward day by day in the experience of the power of the death and resurrection of Christ.

        (a.) We live through faith, answering the call of God to live a life "on high in Christ Jesus" (cf. Phil. 3:14).

        (b.) The resurrection of Christ influences our lives until that moment when we shall see God face to face.

Conclusion: Like St. Paul we "have been grasped by Christ" (cf. Phil. 3:12) in the sacrament of baptism. Now we live under the influence of his death and resurrection with confidence that we shall grasp Christ in the life of eternal glory.

THE FIFTH SUNDAY OF LENT

Introduction: An encounter with the Pharisees provides the setting for the lesson Our Lord teaches us in the Gospel for today's Mass— that hypocrisy is a great obstacle to grace. Although the Pharisees as a group were addicted to religious formalism, this was not their greatest evil. Religious formalism can be changed and corrected, but hypocrisy, which is allied to spiritual blindness, is a greater spiritual evil, and the spiritual blindness of the majority of the party of the Pharisees was self-inflicted.

I Christ exposed the hypocrisy of the Pharisees.
  A. The Pharisees, in their zeal for the Law, were blinded to their need for Christ.
    1. The Pharisees were zealous for the Law.
      a. The origin of the term "pharisee" is uncertain.
      b. Usually "pharisee" was taken to mean "separated" or "separation"; both meanings apply to the group depicted in the gospels as having been opposed to Christ.
        1.) Those opponents of Christ who were known as "Pharisees" considered themselves to be separated from all other groups within the Jewish community.
          (a.) The Pharisees despised anyone who was ignorant of their fine legal distinctions.
          (b.) The Pharisees avoided people whom they called "sinners."
          (c.) The Sadducees, who denied the resurrection and the existence of angels, were also opposed by the Pharisees.
        2.) The Pharisees were also "separators" in the sense that they made exact legal distinctions in the application of the Law to the practical details of daily life.
          (a.) The Pharisees saw the Law as the center of Jewish life, and they believed that every aspect of life was directed by some detail of the Law.
          (b.) To the Law, the Pharisees added oral traditions to which they gave an importance equal to the Law itself.

(c.) They interpreted the Law in severe terms, and they believed that the oral traditions had to be observed strictly to avoid violations of the Law.

2. The Pharisees were blinded to their need for Christ.

   a. According to the Pharisees, the Law and human traditions alone sufficed for sanctity.

      1.) The Pharisees directed all their attention to the details of legal observance.

      2.) They demanded strict fulfillment of the externals of Jewish observance and did not consider the motives for such observances; interior dispositions were not discussed by the Pharisees.

   b. The Pharisees could not see the need for Christ.

      1.) The human traditions of the Pharisees were destroying their need for God.

         (a.) In the Pharisees' rigidly legal view of life, God's love and mercy were limited.

         (b.) Because of their exact legal observance the Pharisees thought they could make demands on God.

            (i.) The Pharisees believed that their exact observance of the Law would automatically save them.

            (ii.) Refusing to believe that the spiritual life could grow beyond the legal observance, the Pharisees attempted to impede the divine plan for the salvation of mankind through Our Lord.

      2.) The Pharisees thought they could destroy Christ.

         (a.) The Pharisees tried to trap Christ.

            (i.) "They were posing this question to trap him so that they could have something to accuse him of" (John 8:6).

            (ii.) The Pharisees wanted Christ to judge the woman "who had been caught in adultery" (John 8:3).

         (b.) If Christ was merciful to the adulterous woman, the Pharisees would say he was opposed to Moses.

         (c.) If Christ said she deserved death he would be denounced to the Romans, who reserved to themselves the right to inflict capital punishment.

B. Christ exposed the Pharisees as hypocrites.

   1. We must realize that there were very sincere men among

the Pharisees.

a. Nicodemus and Gamaliel, both Pharisees, were sincere in their religious observances.

b. Christ praised the Pharisees for their zeal for the Law and for their concern for purity and spiritual perfection.

2. As a class the Pharisees ignored the more sacred obligations of the Law and insisted on external formalities.

a. The Pharisees brought before Christ and everyone else in the Temple area a woman, saying: "This woman has been caught in the act of adultery" (John 8:2-4).

1.) The Pharisees offered no evidence of her crime.

2.) The Gospel story does not tell how she had been apprehended in her crime.

b. Twice St. John mentions that during this incident Our Lord wrote on the ground (cf. John 8:6, 8).

1.) Christ did this to show that he was aware of their insincerity; he was able to read in their hearts the intention to trap him.

2.) Christ brought the Pharisees face to face with their own conscience.

(a.) "Let the man among you who has no sin be the first to cast a stone at her" (John 8:7).

(b.) Our Lord was asking them if they felt worthy in conscience to sit in judgment on another.

(c.) Conscious of their own sin the Pharisees walked away.

II Today the spirit of the Pharisees is opposed to the spirit of Christ.

A. In certain circles the spirit of the Pharisees remains.

1. Today the spirit of the Pharisees can be seen in the attempt to cover oneself with the mask of justice.

a. This is the attitude of one who marshals laws and legal precedents to justify his actions.

1.) Naturally there are times when the use of law is necessary.

2.) But one who feels the prick of conscience often resorts to the law to avoid admitting his sin, to save face, or to rationalize his position.

b. Such a person pretends he is living a virtuous life.

2. The spirit of the Pharisees is present when, in the performance of religious deeds, one is prompted to act for self rather

than for God.
  a. This spirit usually appears when selfish motives direct
     one's public prayers, fasts, or acts of charity.
       1.) The motive for religious deeds may be the desire to
           win the esteem of one's neighbors.
       2.) A person's heart is far from God if his only concern is
           his popularity; he wants people to like him or to praise
           him when such respect is not deserved.
  b. An egocentric approach to religion is never part of a sin-
     cere love of God and neighbor.
       1.) An egocentric approach to religion indicates a love of
           self.
       2.) It may contain an implicit denial of one's need for
           grace.
B. The spirit of the Pharisees is opposed to the spirit of Christ.
  1. The pharisaical approach to life fails to admit one's need for
     redemption.
     a. This approach denies the need for an interior life of prayer
        and sacrifice, both of which are necessary for salvation.
     b. It fails to admit that one is a sinner.
          1.) With such an attitude one cannot hear the call of God
              to conversion.
          2.) The result is failure to cooperate with the grace of
              God.
  2. Christ calls all people to share in his life and to grow in it.
     a. The modern pharisaical spirit denies the need to grow in
        the life of Christ.
     b. This spirit sets its own limits on the mercy and love of
        Christ.

Conclusion: As we think of the Gospel for today we realize that we
are standing before Christ. We can identify with the Pharisees who
walked away from Christ when they saw themselves as they really
were. On the other hand, like the adulterous woman, we can stand
before Christ and admit we need him. Then hear Christ say: "You
may go. But from now on avoid this sin" (John 8:11).

THE FIFTH SUNDAY OF LENT

(This year the priest may use for the Gospel of today's
Mass the reading from John 11:1-45 included in Year A.)

Introduction: Many interesting questions could be asked about the details in this account of Christ's restoration of the dead Lazarus to life. However, all of the facts given to us in St. John's Gospel serve to teach one lesson: The sole reason for the miraculous resurrection of Lazarus was to give glory to God.

I The glorification of God was the purpose of Christ's restoration to life of the dead Lazarus.
- A. Our Lord, hearing that Lazarus was sick, said: "This sickness is not to end in death; rather it is for God's glory, that through it the Son of God may be glorified" (John 11:4).
  - 1. The Jewish people believed that God revealed his glory by his deeds.
    - a. The Old Testament presents the created universe as a manifestation of the glory of God (cf. Ps. 104).
    - b. God intervened in the history of the Israelites and revealed his glory.
      - 1.) To the Israelites the Exodus experience was a manifestation of God's glory (cf. Exodus 14:18; 16:7).
      - 2.) The restoration of the Israelites to their homeland was a manifestation of God's glory (cf. Pss. 98, 103).
  - 2. The details of the account of Lazarus' resurrection emphasize the action of God.
    - a. Christ seemed to ignore the request implicit in the message he received from Martha and Mary (cf. John 11:1-4).
      - 1.) After receiving the message that Lazarus was sick, Christ remained where he was for two days (cf. John 11:6).
      - 2.) Christ insisted that he delay his journey so see Lazarus because as he said: "Lazarus is dead. For your sakes I am glad I was not there, that you may come to believe" (John 11:15).
      - 3.) Christ had good reasons for his delay: that those close to him would believe (cf. John 11:15) and that God would be glorified (cf. John 11:4).
    - b. The detail informing us that Lazarus had been dead four days serves to illustrate the action of God (cf. John 11:17, 39).
      - 1.) At the time of Christ it was commonly believed by the Jewish people that the soul of a dead person lingered for three days near the body it had inhabited.

2.) On the fourth day there was no hope of resuscitation by natural means.

3.) On the fourth day Christ performed the miracle of the raising of Lazarus; according to the Jewish belief at the time, this could have been done only by the power of God, for no other explanation was possible.

4.) Christ's action manifested God's glory.

B. This miracle also prefigured the glorification of God by the resurrection of Christ.

1. The miracle of the resurrection of Lazarus was a sign of the coming resurrection of Christ.

a. The details of the account of the resurrection of Lazarus are signs of the coming resurrection of Christ.

1.) Christ did not hurry to the home of his friends; neither friend nor foe could force Christ to action, for his life and works were determined by God alone.

2.) At the tomb of Lazarus Christ prayed: "Father, I thank you for having heard me. I know that you always hear me but I have said this for the sake of the crowd, that they may believe that you sent me" (John 11:41, 42).

3.) This miracle, like the resurrection of Christ, forced individuals either to profess their faith in Christ or to declare their opposition to Christ.

b. The words of Christ indicated his future resurrection.

1.) In the conversation with Martha, Christ said: "I am the resurrection and the life" (John 11:25).

(a.) Christ was life because he possessed life from all eternity as the Son of God.

(b.) As man Christ was life; as the master of life he gave abundant life to those who accepted him in faith, and endowed people with the power to live by him (cf. John 5:26; 10:10; 17:2, 6:53-58).

2.) Christ was the resurrection.

(a.) Christ said that he would lose his life only "to take it up again" (John 10:17 f.).

(b.) Christ was the life-giving spirit after his resurrection (cf. I Cor. 15:45); he who gave life to Lazarus declared: ". . . whoever believes in me though he should die, will come to life; and whoever is alive and believes in me will never die" (John 11:26).

2. The resurrection of Christ glorified God.

    a. By his resurrection Christ entered into his glory.

        1.) This was the glory of God that Christ had enjoyed; this glory was given to him before the foundation of the world (cf. John 17:24).

            (a.) It was the glory that belonged to Christ as the Son of God.

            (b.) God has raised Christ from the dead and had given him divine glory (cf. I Peter 1:21).

        2.) Christ radiated this glory in his risen body.

    b. The glory of the risen Christ glorified God as the source of holiness, power, and life for others.

        1.) In the Old Testament the glory of God was the source of holiness, power, and life for the Israelites.

        2.) The resurrection of Christ was the cause of the new creation (cf. II Cor. 4:6).

            (a.) This new creation glorified God through the resurrection of Christ.

            (b.) This new creation was purity, light, holiness, power, and life (cf. Acts 7:55; 22:11; II Cor. 3:10; 4:6).

II The account of the resurrection of Lazarus gives us a realization of our dignity and our honor.

    A. The resurrection of Lazarus is a promise of our resurrection.

        1. The resurrection of Lazarus is a proof of the power of Christ to give life.

            a. "Lord, if you were here my brother would never have died. . . . Your brother will rise again . . . whoever believes in me, though he should die, will come to life; and whoever is alive and believes in me will never die" (John 11:23-27).

                1.) Our Lord confirmed Martha's faith in the resurrection.

                2.) Christ added that the source of the final resurrection is to be found in him.

            b. Physical death is the one experience all men will share, but faith in Christ will bring men back to life in the resurrection.

        2. At the sound of Christ's voice, Lazarus comes from the tomb.

            a. This is proof of the truth of which Christ had spoken: He had the power to restore life.

            b. The resurrection of Lazarus confirmed Martha's faith and

our faith, too, in our resurrection on the last day.
   B. It is our resurrection that is the source of our dignity and our
      honor.
      1. Our resurrection is the source of our dignity.
         a. Now we realize that we are indeed citizens of heaven.
         b. We are risen with Christ (cf. Phil. 3:20; Col. 3:1).
            1.) We wait with confidence for that moment when Christ
               will take us with him (cf. John 14:3).
            2.) We live as citizens of heaven, proving ourselves inno-
               cent children of God, shining like stars in the sky (cf.
               Phil. 2:15).
      2. Our resurrection with Christ is our honor.
         a. Others see our good works and glorify God (cf. Matt.
            5:16).
            1.) We stand before the world, reminding it of God's mer-
               cy, goodness, and love.
            2.) We lead others to adore and praise God.
         b. Our honorable pride extends even to our bodies, by
            which we glorify God (cf. I Cor. 6:15, 19).
            1.) To glorify God we suffer for Christ in our bodies (cf. I
               Peter 4:16).
            2.) We fulfill our mission in life by seeking the glory of
               God (cf. John 7:18).
            3.) We place our honor in the hands of God (cf. John 8:50
               and Luke 23:46).

Conclusion: Here at Mass we are witnesses to the resurrection
of Lazarus as told in the Gospel. We are witnesses to the resurrection of Christ in the sacrifice of the Mass. We have the promise of
our resurrection in the words and actions of Christ. May this cause
us, who have heard and seen, to put our faith in him.

OPTIONAL MASS FOR THE FIFTH WEEK OF LENT

Introduction: As we read the Responsorial Psalm for today's Mass,
we become aware that it was written with mixed emotions. A spirit
of anxiety dominated the psalmist as he described the actions of the
group of men who pursued him and who were determined to destroy him. But this was replaced by a feeling of confidence and
peace as the psalmist recalled his innocence and prayed for a

greater awareness of the presence of God.

I The psalmist longed for the divine gift of a greater awareness of the presence of God.
   A. The psalmist believed in the presence of God.
      1. Following the tradition of the Israelites, the psalmist knew he was in the presence of God.
         a. The history of the Israelites was a manifestation of God to his people.
            1.) God revealed himself to the Israelites by storm, fire, and wind; these are mentioned frequently in the Old Testament as signs of God's presence.
            2.) God lived among the Israelites; he filled the tent of the Ark of the Covenant with his glory (cf. Exodus 40:34).
         b. During Israel's history God revealed his presence to special individuals.
            1.) God revealed his presence to the patriarchs (cf. Gen. 17:7; 26:24; 28:15).
            2.) God revealed his presence to the individuals to whom he confided the care of Israel, e.g., Moses, Joshua, kings, and prophets (cf. Exodus 3:21; Josh. 1:5; Judg. 6:16; I Sam. 3:19).
      2. The psalmist expressed his belief in the presence of God.
         a. The psalmist used poetic language to express his faith in God's presence.
            1.) "Hear O Lord . . . attend to my outcry . . . I call upon you . . . incline your ear to me" (cf. Ps. 17:1,6).
            2.) The psalmist also spoke of finding refuge at God's right hand and in the "shadow of your wings" (cf. Ps. 17:7,8).
         b. The psalmist believed that after his trials he would enjoy the presence of God.
            1.) The psalmist was certain he would be declared innocent by God (cf. Ps. 17:3,4,5).
            2.) The psalmist knew that God would protect him (cf. Ps. 17:8).
            3.) The psalmist believed that he would enjoy the presence of God (cf. Ps. 17:15).
   B. The psalmist desired to possess the divine gift: a keen awareness of God's presence.
      1. A keen awareness of God's presence was a divine gift.

   a. The psalmist knew that God always took the initiative in
      saving his people (cf. Ps. 17:7).
   b. The psalmist knew that God's protection was a gift and a
      sign of his presence (cf. Ps. 17:8-9).
2. The psalmist desired to possess the gift of God's presence.
   a. The Old Testament directed the devout Israelite to seek the
      presence of God in confident prayer and sincere worship.
      1.) In Psalm 17 the psalmist expressed his confidence by
         his frequent prayers (cf. Ps. 17:1,6,7,13) for divine help.
      2.) The psalmist offered to God the worship of a faithful
         heart (cf. Ps. 17:1,3,5).
   b. God manifested his presence to those Israelites who in-
      voked him in trials and sought him with a humble and
      contrite heart.
      1.) When the psalmist was distressed he sought God.
      2.) The psalmist recognized his dependence upon God's
         help.

II We must search for the presence of God.
   A. We believe in the presence of God.
      1. We believe that God's presence is manifested in creation.
         a. God is the Creator who is present to all creatures (Wis.
            11:25; Rom. 1:20).
         b. The creation of the human race manifests the presence of
            God because he said: "Let us make man in our image, af-
            ter our likeness" (Gen. 1:26).
      2. We believe that God is present in the liturgy.
         a. In the liturgical celebration we gather together to pray:
            "Where two or three are gathered in my name, there am I
            in their midst" (Matt. 18:29).
         b. Throughout the liturgy the Spirit of God communicates
            his love and manifests the abiding presence of Christ (cf.
            John 13:34).
   B. We must strive to develop our awareness of the presence of
      God.
      1. In our daily work we must try to be increasingly aware of the
         presence of God.
         a. We can think of God's presence as we prepare to leave our
            homes to go to work.
         b. While we work we can recall that we are in the presence
            of God.

1.) The doctor and the nurse can think of God present to them as they use their science and skills to restore the order God created in the human body.

2.) Teachers can use the classroom to be reminded of God's presence when, teaching the social sciences, they recall the fatherhood of God and the brotherhood of man; history can be viewed as the unfolding of divine providence; science is the account of God's government of the world; literature recounts the influence of God in the lives of people; mathematics reminds one of the infinity of God.

3.) As the laborer contributes to the welfare of others by his trade, he can see his role in God's providence.

4.) Parents can see their role in divine providence, recognizing that they are the instruments of God as they guide their children.

2. Participating in the liturgy, we strive to grow in our consciousness of the presence of God.

   a. As we listen to the readings of the Mass we try to realize more and more that God is speaking to us personally.

   b. We strive to perfect our faith so that there is an increase in our awareness of the presence of the Spirit of God who forms us in the image of Christ.

     1.) The Holy Spirit present in us by grace makes the prayer of Christ our prayer (cf. Rom. 8:15).

     2.) The Holy Spirit guides us to a more intimate sharing of the Paschal Mystery.

     3.) The Holy Spirit enacts in our lives the life of Christ (cf. I John 3:24).

Conclusion: We, like the psalmist, seek the presence of God. More aware of his abiding presence we face life with greater confidence; each deed we perform is sanctified and we are led to a more intimate union with God. Each one in faith is able to say that in eternity: ". . . on waking, I shall be content in your presence" (Ps. 17:15).

MONDAY OF THE FIFTH WEEK OF LENT

Introduction: The Responsorial Psalm of today's Mass is a classic work of religious literature. One author has said that if all other books of religious prayer and instruction were destroyed, leaving only the twenty-third Psalm, we would have sufficient material to lift the human spirit to God. This psalm is a perfect picture of the goodness and providence of God.

I The psalmist used two poetic images to describe the goodness of God.

   A. God was pictured by the psalmist as a shepherd who cares for his sheep.

      1. The use of the shepherd to symbolize God was a fairly frequent practice in the Old Testament.

         a. This was due to the traditions of the Israelites, which were rooted in a nomadic, pastoral civilization.

         b. The Hebrews thought of the shepherd as a leader and as a companion.

            1.) The shepherd led and guided his flock.

            2.) The shepherd also accompanied his flock as it moved from pasture to pasture.

      2. The poetic image of a shepherd was applied to God's dealings with his people.

         a. As the shepherd cared for his sheep, God provided for his people.

            1.) God does not forcefully drive his people but rather directs them by gentle guidance.

            2.) The careful shepherd leads his flock to good pastures and restful waters when the heat of the sun is fierce; God leads his people to himself where he refreshes them from the heat of temptation.

         b. God, like the shepherd, protected the lives of those in his care.

            1.) At times the shepherd had to lead his flock through dark valleys, the hiding places of the wild beasts that were natural enemies of the sheep.

               (a.) The shepherd had a rod, a weapon he used to defend the sheep.

               (b.) The sheep were secure under the protection of the shepherd.

            2.) God's providence protected his people.

               (a.) God defended his people from their enemies.

               (b.) As long as the Israelites remained under the protection of God they were secure and free from anxiety.

B. To symbolize God's goodness the psalmist likened him to a host who offers hospitality.

    1. A guest was secure in the hospitality offered by his host.

        a. Among the ancient nomadic people hospitality was an important virtue.

            1.) Travel in the desert was difficult and often dangerous.

            2.) People shared what they had with the traveler to refresh him or to protect him from the elements and, at times, from his enemies.

        b. God's goodness gave security to the Israelites.

            1.) God assumed responsibility for the welfare of Israel.

            2.) It was evident to other nations that God protected Israel.

    2. A host provided for his guests.

        a. A host anointed with oil the guests at his table; God filled the hearts of the Israelites with joy, which was symbolized by the anointing with oil (cf. Ps. 23:4).

        b. A host prepared his table to satisfy his guests; God provided for the physical welfare of Israel and provided for all its needs (cf. Ps. 23:3).

II Christ is our shepherd and host.

    A. Christ is our shepherd.

        1. It is as the good shepherd that Christ reveals to us the goodness of the heavenly father.

            a. Christ is the good shepherd sent by the heavenly Father to the lost sheep (cf. Matt. 15:24; 10:6; Luke 19:10).

                1.) Christ is to seek out and save the sheep that are lost.

                2.) Christ is to gather the sheep into one flock under the guidance of one shepherd.

                    (a.) The flock may be harassed, dispersed, and threatened by thieves and wolves.

                    (b.) Christ, the good shepherd, frees his sheep, leads them to green pastures and cool water, and protects them.

            b. The sheep know their good shepherd.

                1.) Christ is the shepherd who saves the flock committed to his care.

                2.) Christ, the good shepherd, calls his sheep by name, and they follow him.

        2. Christ is the good shepherd who lays down his life for his flock.

    a. During these last days of Lent this lesson is impressed upon us.

        1.) We see Christ in his suffering and death, which he freely accepts.

        2.) Christ suffers and dies for our welfare; he protects us not with a rod, but with his cross.

    b. In the death of the good shepherd we find life.

        1.) By the death of Christ we are led to a more perfect life of grace and virtue.

        2.) We live a life of love founded on the mutual love of Christ and his heavenly Father.

        3.) The sheep that are called by Christ come from Israel and all other nations to form one sheepfold which will last forever.

           (a.) This one fold is maintained by divine love.

           (b.) In this love the fold has assurance of eternal life.

B. Christ is our host who invites us to share his life.

    1. Christ invites us to share his sacred banquet.

        a. We are pilgrims, traveling through this world in need of nourishment.

        b. Christ invites us to share the banquet he has prepared.

           1.) "Come to me. . . . My heart is moved with pity for the crowd" (Matt. 11:28; Mark 8:2).

           2.) "The bread that I will give is my flesh for the life of the world" (John 6:51).

    2. Christ invites us to share his eternal glory.

        a. "I will not leave you orphaned; I will come back to you. . . . You see me as one who has life, and you will have life. On that day you will know that I am in my Father, and you in me and I in you" (John 14:18-20).

        b. "I am indeed going to prepare a place for you, and then I shall come back to take you with me, that where I am you also may be" (John 14:3).

Conclusion: Like a good shepherd, Christ watches and protects us as we live on earth. By his cross Christ defends and protects us from the attacks of our spiritual enemies. By the Holy Eucharist, Christ nourishes us until that moment when we "shall dwell in the house of the Lord for years to come" (Ps. 23:6).

TUESDAY OF THE FIFTH WEEK OF LENT

Introduction: The Responsorial Psalm for today's Mass is the account of a man who found some purpose in his sufferings. The psalmist suffered from a physical malady, unnamed in the psalm; he was also tormented by his enemies. As he lamented his fate the psalmist paused to reflect on God and his ways. In his moments of reflection the psalmist's belief in God's eternal purpose grew strong, and he saw suffering in its true perspective. The psalmist found peace.

I Suffering taught the psalmist the value of his life.
  A. The psalmist suffered intensely.
    1. The psalmist suffered physical pain.
      a. The psalmist did not describe the nature of his physical illness.
      b. The psalmist used figures of speech to illustrate his physical distress.
        1.) To indicate that he was at the point of extinction, the psalmist likened his physical condition to smoke that is carried away by the wind (cf. Ps. 102:4).
        2.) When he was consumed by fever, the psalmist said it seemed that his bones were being consumed by the fire in a hearth (cf. Ps. 102:4).
        3.) So intense was the pain suffered by the psalmist that he compared his heart to grass dried up by the heat of the summer's sun (cf. Ps. 102:5).
        4.) Pain had destroyed the psalmist's appetite; he could not eat (cf. Ps. 102:5).
    2. The psalmist endured mental suffering.
      a. The psalmist used impressive figures of speech to describe his loneliness.
        1.) The psalmist likened his lonely condition to that of a desert owl that makes its home in deserted places (cf. Ps. 102:7).
        2.) The psalmist compared his feeling of abandonment to the loneliness and grief of a sparrow, sitting alone on a housetop, grieving for its lost mate (cf. Ps. 102:8).
      b. Ridicule increased the suffering in the soul of the psalmist.

        1.) The psalmist had enemies who taunted him by asking why God did not relieve his suffering (cf. Ps. 102:9).

        2.) Some of the scoffers used the psalmist's name as a curse (cf. Ps. 102:9).

      c. Added to his personal sorrow was the humiliation the psalmist shared with his people in exile.

B. From his suffering the psalmist learned the quality of his life.

    1. In suffering the psalmist learned the difference between his life and the eternity of God's providence.

      a. The psalmist paused in his lament to reflect on his life.

      b. In this reflection the psalmist experienced a growth in his awareness of the difference between God and himself.

        1.) The psalmist realized that his life was passing; he would not live permanently on earth (cf. Ps. 102:12, 24).

        2.) Suffering deepened the psalmist's faith in the eternity of God and in God's providence.

          (a.) God was eternal: "... you, O Lord, abide forever, and your name through all generations" (Ps. 102: 13; cf. Ps. 102:27,28).

          (b.) The psalmist learned that God does permit suffering.

    2. In his suffering the psalmist learned that his life could serve others.

      a. After his reflection on God's eternal providence, the psalmist returned to thoughts of his own condition.

        1.) This consideration was not selfish or filled with self-pity.

        2.) This time the psalmist was more concerned with the welfare of others than with his own condition.

      b. The psalmist learned that God noticed human suffering.

        1.) In his sufferings the psalmist prayed with confidence for the restoration of Israel (cf. Ps. 102:14, 15-23).

        2.) Aware of the eternal purpose of God, the psalmist prayed in his sufferings for the future generations of Israelites (cf. Ps. 102:29).

II Enlightened by faith, we learn from our sufferings the intercessory and redemptive value of our lives.

  A. Faith teaches us the value of suffering.

    1. Faith enlightens us about "the mystery of suffering."

      a. Faith teaches us that God does permit suffering.

      1.) This does not mean that either God or we ourselves are to be insensitive to suffering.

      2.) Faith teaches us, that in the providence of God, suffering has a purifying value.

         (a.) As gold is purified in a fire that removes the dross, so is the human spirit purified in suffering.

         (b.) Suffering teaches one patience, humility, and confidence in God, provided one accepts suffering in a spirit of faith and love of God.

   b. In his providence God permits suffering to correct his loving children.

      1.) Suffering is a sign that God's mercy is present in our lives, for in suffering God gives us the opportunity to amend our lives.

      2.) Here again this presupposes that one accepts suffering in faith; without faith in God's purpose, suffering may cause one to grow bitter.

  2. Suffering is also a test to which God subjects us.

   a. Frequently God uses suffering to test the faith of an individual.

   b. During the experience of suffering, one does not always understand its reason or purpose.

      1.) At such times one has to turn to God in confident prayer.

      2.) Only when one looks back on suffering, years after the experience has passed, does one understand why God permitted it.

B. Suffering has an intercessory and redemptive value in our lives.

  1. Suffering has an intercessory value in our lives.

   a. Suffering is offered to God in petition for a grace needed.

   b. Suffering may be offered to ask God for grace for oneself or for another.

      1.) Suffering is offered to God to conform a person to the Divine Will; suffering expiates sin, which is rebellion against God.

      2.) Suffering disposes an individual to receive grace from God.

      3.) Suffering must be accepted in faith, patience, and generosity if one is to receive greater graces from God.

  2. By conforming us to Christ, suffering has a redemptive value in our lives.

   a. Suffering enables us to live our baptismal conformity to the sufferings of Christ.

the sufferings of Christ.

1.) Through suffering we become more aware of our conformity to the sufferings of Christ.

2.) St. Paul is very clear as he teaches us this truth.

  (a.) "... to know how to share in his sufferings by being formed into the pattern of his death" (Phil. 3:10).

  (b.) "Our hope for you is firm because we know that just as you share in the sufferings, so you will share in the consolation" (II Cor. 1:7).

  (c.) "... we carry about in our bodies the dying of Jesus, so that in our bodies the life of Jesus may also be revealed" (II Cor. 4:10).

b. Our suffering contributes to the redemption of souls.

  1.) As Christ offered himself for others, so we who are conformed to him offer ourselves together with him for the spiritual welfare of souls.

  2.) In our suffering we can apply to people in our generation and in our locality the merits of Christ for their salvation.

Conclusion: In our suffering, united to Christ, we pray to the heavenly Father: "O Lord, hear my prayer, and let my cry come to you" (Ps. 102:1).

WEDNESDAY OF THE FIFTH WEEK OF LENT

Introduction: The Responsorial Psalm for today's Mass is a hymn praising and glorifying God. This hymn was sung by three men, Shadrach, Meshach, and Abednego, when they were rescued from a blazing furnace. These three men had refused to adore a golden statue made by King Nebuchadnezzar. To punish the three, who were former administrators of the king, they were cast into a furnace. "But the angel of the Lord went down into the furnace . . . drove the fiery flames out of the furnace . . . the fire in no way touched them or caused them pain or harm" (Dan. 3:49-50).

I. Shadrach, Meshach, and Abednego expressed their faith and love for God by praising him.

  A. The three men were strengthened in their faith and in their love for God.

1. The three men had expressed their faith and love for God by refusing to obey the royal edict to adore a golden statue.
   a. They believed their lives were in the hands of God (cf. Dan. 3:16-18).
   b. Having been cast into the fire, "they walked about in the flames, singing to God and blessing the Lord" (Dan. 3:24).
2. In the furnace the three devout Israelites had an overwhelming experience of God's powerful presence.
   a. God manifested his presence to the three men.
      1.) God sent his angel to protect them from the flames of the fire.
      2.) This confirmed their faith in God and their love for him.
   b. Overwhelmed by this proof of God's presence and power, the three men sang a hymn praising and glorifying God.

B. In a beautiful hymn they expressed their faith and their love for God.
   1. The three were grateful for the gift they had received from God.
      a. They thanked God for effecting their rescue.
      b. The hymn was primarily a song in praise of God.
         1.) Their attention was not focused only on the gift God had granted.
         2.) Their attention was attracted by God himself, of whose greatness they sang.
   2. The three men praised the greatness of God whom they believed and loved.
      a. In their hymn the three men multiplied the phrases that expressed their faith in the greatness of God himself.
         1.) "The God of our fathers. . . your holy and glorious name" (cf. Dan. 3:52).
         2.) "In the temple of your holy glory. . . on the throne of your kingdom" (cf. Dan. 3:53-4).
         3.) "You look in the depths from your throne upon the cherubium . . ." (cf. Dan. 3:55).
      b. The words of this hymn in praise of God are an expression of love for God himself.
         1.) The three men, having experienced a miraculous rescue, became lyrical with joy.
            (a.) Their whole being was filled with joy when God manifested power over the flames.
            (b.) In their joy the thoughts of the rescued men were

transferred from the rescue to the author of their
safety, God himself.

    2.) The hymn is a celebration of the majestic presence of
the all-powerful God.

II We offer our prayer of faith and love in praise of God.

  A. We are aware of the presence of God.

    1. All of nature directs our attention to the greatness of God.

      a. In faith we know that God created all things for his glory:
"The Lord made everything for his own ends. . ." (Prov.
16:4).

      b. The heavens declare the glory of God, as we are reminded
by the psalms (cf. Pss. 8:4; 19:2-3).

    2. Each one of us experiences the greatness of God.

      a. We experience the greatness of God as we vacation in the
mountains, drive to the seashore, or look at a star-filled sky.

      b. We know the greatness of God as we study science; in lit-
erature a book that effectively portrays the development
of its characters or unfolds historical events reveals to us
the goodness and greatness of God.

      c. The greatness and goodness of God touch our lives as we
experience his love and mercy in the events of our daily
lives.

  B. Motivated by faith and love, we praise God.

    1. We are grateful for God's gifts to us, for they assure us of his
presence, mercy, love, and greatness.

    2. Our prayer of praise rises above these gifts, to God himself.

      a. Our prayer of praise is an expression of our faith in God.

        1.) We offer praise to the unseen God.

        2.) By faith we are aware of the overwhelming greatness
of God.

          (a.) In our prayer of praise we recognize God's great-
ness.

          (b.) Our prayer of praise is a confession of our insigni-
ficance before God and of our dependence upon
him.

          (c.) Our faith sharpens our awareness of God, and we
react to this faith by using all of our faculties to
praise him.

      b. Our prayer of praise is an expression of our love for God.

        1.) Our praise of God is an expression of our delight in his
perfection; it expresses our admiration of the divine
goodness.

2.) Our praise of God expresses our love of his benevolence as we fulfill the petition of the Our Father, "Hallowed be thy name."

(a.) Our praise of God expresses our desire that all men honor and respect God.

(b.) In our prayer of praise all creation is caught up in this act of glorifying God.

(i.) Human nature is the mediator for inanimate creation in the act of praising God.

(ii.) Human nature lends its understanding, its love, and its voice to creation so that it may in and through mankind praise God.

3.) Praising God, we express our penitential or contrite love for God as we grieve for the offences we have committed against the divine majesty and goodness.

4.) Our praise of God expresses our grateful love for God's goodness, love, and mercy.

Conclusion: By your marvelous deeds, O Lord, "let them know that you alone are the Lord God, glorious over the whole world" (Dan. 3:45). "Blessed are you in the firmament of heaven, praiseworthy and glorious forever" (Dan. 3:56).

THURSDAY OF THE FIFTH WEEK OF LENT

Introduction: In the Responsorial Psalm for today's Mass there is a brief lesson about Israel's history. Psalm 105, from which the few verses for today's Mass are taken, was an account of the chief events of Israel's history, from the call of Abraham to the time the nation entered the Promised Land.

The six verses of Psalm 105 that are used today indicate the reason for this brief history lesson. The psalm records the favorable events of Israel's history so that all people may seek to serve God.

I The Israelites were reminded that they were to seek God with joy in their hearts.

A. The Israelites were reminded that they were to seek God.

1. To encourage them to seek God, the Israelites were reminded of their history.

a. For the Israelites, the purpose of their history was to remind them, as a nation and as individuals, that they had a
special role in the divine plan.
  1.) The sacred writer recorded the events of Israel's his-
      tory to impress upon the Israelites that they were to
      bring salvation to the world.
  2.) For the Israelites, the interpretation of history was the
      application of its lessons to daily life.
      (a.) By the application of history to his life the Israelite
           entered into history.
      (b.) In this way the Israelite continued the saving
           events of history in his own experience.
b. History for the Israelite was not static.
  1.) For the Israelite, the events of his nation's history were
      not a mere record of the past.
  2.) For the Israelite, history was the continuous offering
      by God of his goodness to men, together with the hu-
      man response to the divine initiative.
2. Recalling the history of his nation, the Israelite was inspired
   to seek God in his life.
   a. The psalmist recalled that it was from the small clan of
      Abraham that God had made his own people.
     1.) It was with this small clan that God made the Covenant.
     2.) God was faithful to his promises, and that small clan
         grew into a great nation.
   b. The psalmist used the history of Abraham's clan to inspire
      the Israelites to seek God.
     1.) The Israelite was one of the few, the remnant, who re-
         turned from the exile.
     2.) Under God's protection that small remnant was to
         grow into a great nation.
     3.) Like his ancestors, the Israelite sought God by fulfill-
         ing the terms of the Covenant.
B. The Israelite was to seek God with joy.
   1. The joy of the Israelite was founded on his confidence that
      he was not seeking God in vain.
      a. History taught the Israelite that his search for God would
         be rewarded.
      b. By his knowledge of his nation's history, the Israelite was
         united to his nation, and he identified with its experience.
   2. The nation rejoiced in God's saving deeds for the people.

  a. The individual Israelite realized that he had a share in the saving actions that God performed for his people.

  b. The individual Israelite rejoiced in the fact that God touched his daily life.

   1.) The individual Israelite was a participant in God's continuing saving action.

   2.) Day by day, as he remained faithful to the Covenant, the individual Israelite rejoiced in his union with God.

II We are to seek God with joy.

 A. We are to seek God.

  1. "To seek God" means that we strive to develop our consciousness of God's presence.

   a. We believe that God is present everywhere.

    1.) We believe that God is present to each of his creatures by his power, his essence, and his presence.

    2.) It is God's action, present to all creatures, that sustains and governs all things.

   b. We strive to increase our consciousness of God's presence in the world.

    1.) We try to see God present in nature.

    2.) We try to see God present in the liturgy.

    3.) We try to see God present in all the events of our lives.

  2. We strive to increase our consciousness of the presence of God in our souls.

   a. We believe that God is present by grace in our souls.

    1.) By grace God elevates us to a supernatural life.

    2.) By grace God wishes to share with us his eternal happiness.

   b. We strive to develop our consciousness of the divine presence.

    1.) The effort to seek God must be constant.

     (a.) This effort is our frequent prayer, offered to God who is dwelling in our souls.

     (b.) This effort is our act of faith, seeking union with God in all the events of our lives.

     (c.) This effort is our love of God, accepting his Will as it is revealed in the events of our lives.

    2.) The effort to seek God must be sincere.

     (a.) This sincerity is our love for God himself.

     (b.) This sincerity is the love for our neighbors because

we see God present in them.

(c.) The search for God must be without compromise.
B. The search for God must be made in a spirit of joy.

1. Joy arises in the soul because of the presence of God (cf. Phil. 4:4-5).

   a. We realize that we cannot fulfill our desire for an intimate union with God overnight.

   b. With joy we make the effort, using every opportunity to make acts of faith in God's presence within our hearts.

2. The spirit of joy grows within the soul.

   a. It is an abiding joy in the deep recesses of the soul.

      1.) Yes, such a soul does experience sorrow and pain, disappointments and contradictions.

      2.) The spirit of joy allows one to accept negative experiences joyfully because they contribute to one's spiritual growth and to the spiritual welfare of others.

   b. We contribute to this growth of joy in our souls.

      1.) We examine our values by asking, "What fills my mind? Where are my thoughts?"

      2.) When we make the conscious effort to allow God to fill our minds and when we try to turn our thoughts to him, we are seeking God with joy.

Conclusion: We recall our experiences in life; we remember all that God has allowed us to know and to feel, and joy fills our hearts. God has manifested himself to us through these events. In the present moment we seek God with joy. "Rejoice in the Lord always: I say it again. Rejoice" (Phil. 4:4).

FRIDAY OF THE FIFTH WEEK OF LENT

Introduction: Today the Responsorial Psalm, Psalm 18, sings of the joy and triumph of a king. Many commentators have raised questions about this psalm. Its origin, its historical facts, its literary style, and its author have all been subjects of discussion.

However, these same commentators call attention to verse 2 of Psalm 18: "I love you, O Lord." It has been noted that the unusual Hebrew verb employed in this verse has a nuance that indicates a deep and fervent affection for God.

I In response to God's goodness the psalmist lived a life of love for God.

  A. God was generous to the psalmist.

    1. God had protected the psalmist.

      a. At one time the psalmist was in great peril (cf. Ps. 18:5-7).

      b. God intervened to protect him (cf. Ps. 18:8-20).

    2. God granted the psalmist victory in war.

      a. God had protected the psalmist during his preparations for war (cf. Ps. 18:32-35).

      b. With the help of God the psalmist defeated his enemies (cf. Ps. 18:36-39).

  B. In a spirit of gratitude the psalmist filled his life with love for God.

    1. Gratitude was a quality of the psalmist's love for God.

      a. Motivated by love, the psalmist sought to express his appreciation for God's gifts.

        1.) The psalmist appreciated what God had generously done for him.

        2.) The psalmist realized that he did not merit the gifts he had received from God.

      b. The practical expression of the psalmist's love for God was living according to the Law.

    2. A sincere love for God motivated the psalmist in his observance of the Law.

      a. The psalmist kept the Law of God.

        1.) "For I kept the ways of the Lord and was not disloyal to my God" (Ps. 18:22).

        2.) "For his ordinances were all present to me, and his statutes I put not from me" (Ps. 18:23).

      b. Love for God motivated the psalmist.

        1.) "But I was wholehearted toward him, and I was on my guard against guilt" (Ps. 18:24).

          (a.) The psalmist was sincere in his love for God.

          (b.) The psalmist was vigilant lest he offend God.

        2.) The psalmist prayed that he might remain faithful to God (cf. Ps. 18:7).

          (a.) Love for God enlightened the psalmist to the dangers of his personal weaknesses.

          (b.) Loving God as he did, the psalmist did not wish to offend God by his human fraility.

(c.) The psalmist prayed that his love for God would sustain him in his observance of the Law.

II Our lives are an expression of our love for God.
    A. Our lives, like the life of Christ, are dedicated to the heavenly Father.
        1. Motivated by love, Christ dedicates himself to the heavenly Father.
           a. The life of Christ can be judged in the light of his dedication to God the Father.
               1.) From the beginning of his life Our Lord expresses the purpose of his actions: "I have come to do your will, O God" (cf. Heb. 10:5,7).
               2.) "I always do what pleases him" (cf. John 8:29).
           b. At the end of his life Our Lord mentions the purpose of his sufferings: ". . . the world must know that I love the Father and do as the Father has commanded me. Come, then! Let us be on our way" (cf. John 14:31).
               1.) Christ promptly goes to his sufferings.
               2.) Christ is willing to suffer so the world may know of his perfect love for the heavenly Father.
        2. Our love for God is expressed by our dedication to his service.
           a. In the sacrament of baptism we are dedicated to the service of God.
               1.) Love for God is infused into our souls at baptism.
               2.) From the beginning of our supernatural life in baptism, we dedicate ourselves to the service of God.
           b. Throughout our lives the grace of baptism grows as we perfect our love for God.
               1.) Animated by love for God, we follow the commandments.
               2.) Love for God motivates our fidelity to our vocation.
                   (a.) We strive to please God by our conduct, for pleasing him is the purpose of our vocation.
                   (b.) Our love for God is manifested by allowing him to influence the events of our life. (Of course, it is understood that we take virtuous care of our life and make prudent provision for our future.)
    B. Holy Communion is an opportunity for us to renew our dedication to the service of God.

1. Prompted by love for God we say: "To do your will, O my God, is my delight, and your law is within my heart" (Ps. 40:9).
   a. The liturgy allows us to pause after Holy Communion to reflect on God's love for us.
   b. In these meditations we are to respond to God's love for us.
      1.) This response is our willingness to love God by accepting his Will for us.
      2.) Loving God, we review his Law and dedicate ourselves to its observance.
2. Our dedication to the observance of God's Law is not to be exact merely for the sake of exactness.
   a. An overly exact observance of the Law of God can be pharisaical and empty (cf. Matt. 11:18-19; Luke 7:33-34).
   b. Love motivates our rededication to the service of God.
      1.) The service of God, motivated by love for God, is the external expression of our faith and confidence in God.
      2.) Love for God is the center from which flows zeal for the kingdom of God and the love of neighbor.

Conclusion: Love for God gives life and spirit to our works. Love for God enables us to realize the purpose of our creation—the praise of God—by doing his Will. Loving God in all things, we may at the end of life look over our years and proclaim: "I have kept the ways of the Lord and was not disloyal to my God" (Ps. 18:22).

SATURDAY OF THE FIFTH WEEK OF LENT

Introduction: The Responsorial Psalm for today's Mass, taken from the prophet Jeremiah, was a hymn of joy that celebrated the homecoming of the exiles. The triumphal procession of the returning exiles was a source of joy to the Jewish people and to the inhabitants of foreign nations who witnessed it.

The return of the repatriates reaffirmed God's protection of his people. God had conquered the enemies of the Israelites. God had granted salvation to his people. God had confirmed the hope Israel had placed in him.

I The return of the "remnant" justified Israel's hope in God.
   A. Israel's hope in God's Promises had been challenged by the exile of the nation.

1. Israel has placed its hope in the Promises made by God to Abraham.
    a. God had made the Promises to Abraham.
        1.) "I will make of you a great nation, and I will bless you; I will make your name great, so that you will be a blessing. I will bless those who bless you and curse those who curse you. All the communities of the earth shall find blessing in you" (Gen. 12:2-3).
        2.) "To your descendants I will give this land" (Gen. 12:7).
        3.) "Look up at the sky and count the stars, if you can, just so, he added, shall your descendants be" (Gen. 15:5).
    b. Israel hoped these Promises would be fulfilled by God.
        1.) Israel had placed its hope in God, who could not deceive his people.
        2.) Israel looked to the day when it would enjoy the blessings contained in the Promises.
2. This hope had been challenged by the national experiences of Israel.
    a. The exile was a devastating experience.
        1.) The Israelites were desolate as they saw their homes demolished by a reckless enemy.
        2.) With aching hearts they realized that the glorious heir promised to Abraham had not appeared.
        3.) The Israelites were deported from the land that had been promised to them as their possession.
    b. The hope Israel placed in God was tested.
        1.) It seemed that God had closed his heart to the Israelites.
        2.) The Israelites had been expecting a glorious future; now they were defeated by their enemy; they had no status among the nations of the world; they were exiles, and it seemed that not even God cared for them.
B. The return of the "remnant" from exile proved that Israel had not hoped in God in vain.
    1. The name "remnant" was given to the small group of Jewish people who survived the trials of the exile.
        a. This small group of people endured the suffering of the exile as a purification of their souls.
        b. They were the people who led religious lives.
            1.) The "remnant" was the group that was faithful to God.
            2.) The "remnant" of Israel was identified with the pure of heart.

2. The "remnant" confirmed Israel's hope in God.
   a. God had provided for his people.
      1.) The presence of physically handicapped people in the
          line of march was a sign that God had released his peo-
          ple (cf. Jer. 31:8).
          (a.) Physically these people were not able to defeat
               their captors.
          (b.) Only God could have liberated them.
      2.) The level road over which the "remnant" marched
          was a sign that God's care for Israel had made the re-
          turn possible (cf. Jer. 31:9).
      3.) The use of the shepherd as a figure for God revealed
          God's salvific action and his love for Israel (cf. Jer.
          31:10).
   b. The "remnant" was the depository of the Promises.
      1.) From this group would come the Messiah.
      2.) It was the "remnant" which sustained the hope of a
          great and glorious nation.
      3.) From the "remnant" would spring an Israel that would
          be faithful to God.

II The return of the "remnant" from exile stimulates our hope.
   A. The "remnant" of the Old Testament is a symbol of all those
      who will be saved on the last day.
      1. This "remnant" will be realized in the Church of the New
         Testament.
         a. In the Old Testament the "remnant" looks to the future.
            1.) Because the "remnant" is to be purified, it will share
                the holiness of God.
                (a.) "He who remains in Zion and he that is left in Jeru-
                     salem will be called holy. . ." (Isa. 4:3).
                (b.) "Holy, holy, holy is the Lord of hosts! they cried
                     one to the other" (Isa. 6:3).
            2.) This community gathers around the Messiah and by its
                faith depends on God (cf. Isa. 10:20-21).
         b. The "remnant" has a future mission.
            1.) The "remnant" is to bring salvation to Israel.
            2.) Through the "remnant" the pagan world will receive a
                share in the salvation of Israel.
      2. In the New Testament the Church is the "remnant."
         a. The Church is purified by the redemptive action of Christ:

"Christ loved the church. He gave himself up for her to make her holy, purifying her in the bath of water by the power of the word, to present to himself a glorious church, holy and immaculate, without stain or wrinkle or anything of that sort" (Eph. 5:25-27).

   b. The Church gathers around Christ and through him receives the divine life of grace.

   c. The Church has a mission to all people of every generation and in all places.

      1.) It is in the Church and through her mission that the divine Promises are fulfilled.

      2.) In the Church and through her mission, the grace of God continues to prepare souls to be the "remnant" on the last day (cf. Rom. 11:5).

B. Our hope is stimulated as it looks to the future.

  1. Our hope looks to the future coming of Christ.

   a. "Then men will see the Son of Man coming in the clouds with great power and glory" (Mark 13:26).

   b. "Men of Galilee, they said, why do you stand here looking up at the skies? This Jesus who has been taken from you will return, just as you saw him go up into the heavens" (Acts 1:11).

  2. Faith is the stimulus of our hope.

   a. We believe that Christ is the fulfillment of the ancient Promises.

      1.) The coming of Christ inaugurated the kingdom of God on earth.

      2.) Citizenship in this kingdom is faith expressing its hope in the death and resurrection of Christ.

   b. As he fulfills the ancient Promises, Christ gives us promises for the future: "I for my part declare to you, you are 'Rock' and on this rock I will build my church, and the jaws of death shall not prevail against it" (Matt. 16:18).

   c. Our hope is based on the abiding presence of Christ in his Church.

      1.) "And know that I am with you always, until the end of the world!" (Matt. 28:20).

      2.) The glory of Christ is invisibly present in the Church (cf. II Cor. 3:18ff.; II Cor. 4:18; Rom. 8:24-25).

Conclusion: "Rise up. Let us go to Zion, to the Lord, our God" (Jer. 31:6).

PASSION SUNDAY
(Palm Sunday)

The Procession with the Palms
(This year the priest may choose to read the
Gospel of Luke 19:28-40.)

Introduction: The life of Christ is about to end as it began. When Our Lord was born the angels sang: "Glory to God in high heaven, peace on earth to those on whom his favor rests" (Luke 2:14). As Our Lord enters Jerusalem for the last time the people shout: "Blessed be he who comes as king in the name of the Lord! Peace in heaven and glory in the highest" (Luke 19:38).

Both of these joyful hymns are repeated as we form today's procession. In this ceremony—blessing the palms and walking in procession—we pay homage to Christ our King.

I In the city of Jerusalem Christ establishes his kingdom.
  A. The people of Jerusalem celebrate the coming of Christ as king.
    1. The disciples treat Christ like a king.
       a. "They led the animal to Jesus and laying their cloaks on it, helped him mount. They spread their cloaks on the roadway as he moved along" (Luke 19:35-36).
          1.) The disciples pay regal honors to Christ (cf. II Kings 9:13).
          2.) Christ rides into Jerusalem mounted on a donkey.
       b. Christ comes into the city of Jerusalem as the messiahking.
          1.) Historically the donkey was the mount of a king who came in peace; horses were used by warriors for combat and conquest.
          2.) This picture of Christ mounted on a donkey contrasts with the picture of men who prefer to ride on horses (cf. Ps. 20:8-9).
    2. This is the first time Christ has allowed the people to proclaim him king.
       a. In his public life Our Lord has avoided the title of king.
          1.) Christ is not opposed to the temporal power of the civil authorities.

        2.) Christ forbade the demoniacs to call him the messiah; when the people wanted to make him king, Christ disappeared from them.

    b. "On his approach to the descent of Mount Olivet, the entire crowd of disciples began to rejoice and praise God loudly for the display of power they had seen, saying: Blessed be he who comes as king in the name of the Lord! Peace in heaven and glory in the highest" (Luke 19:37-38).

        1.) Now Our Lord is greeted as king.

        2.) The peace and salvation promised by God as the gifts of the messianic king are announced.

        3.) The miracles of Christ have manifested the divine power through which the name of God is glorified.

B. In the city of Jerusalem, Christ inaugurates his rule over human hearts.

    1. Christ fulfills his prophecy.

      a. "So must the Son of Man be lifted up, that all who believe may have eternal life in him" (John 3:14-15).

      b. "The hour has come for the Son of Man to be glorified.... But it was for this that I came to this hour. Father, glorify your name! . . . and I—once I am lifted up from the earth —will draw all men to myself" (John 12:23-32).

    2. In Jerusalem Christ gains control of his kingdom.

      a. Throughout history Jerusalem has been the center of the national life of the people of God.

      b. Christ enters Jerusalem to establish the kingdom of God among the new people of God.

        1.) Christ establishes this kingdom not by the force of arms, but by the persuasion of love.

        2.) Christ establishes the kingdom of God to enrich men with divine life.

          (a.) Christ empties himself that we may be rich in him: "Of his fullness we have all had a share" (John 1:16).

          (b.) Christ gives his life that we may have life because of him (cf. John 6:57).

II We praise Christ the King.

    A. Christ reigns as king in the heavenly Jerusalem.

      1. Christ enters the glory of the heavenly Jerusalem.

        a. By his passion and death Christ corrects the messianic

ideas of his disciples, which are nationalistic and worldly.
   b. Rising from the tomb, the glorious Christ enters his heavenly kingdom.
2. From the glory of the heavenly Jerusalem, Christ reigns.
   a. The heavenly Jerusalem now supplants the old earthly
   Jerusalem.
      1.) The heavenly Jerusalem is the heiress of the Promises
      (Gal. 4:24-31).
      2.) The heavenly Jerusalem is the home of the new Tem-
      ple (cf. Heb. 9:24; 9:11 ff).
   b. Christ reigns for the welfare of all people.
      1.) The reign of Christ is not of this world (cf. John 18:36).
         (a.) Christ is the king of justice and the priestly king
         (cf. Ps. 45:4; Ps. 104:4).
         (b.) The kingdom of Christ is not a human monarchy
         limited to one nation and governing one people.
      2.) Christ reigns in heaven for the benefit of all.
         (a.) Christ enters heaven "that he might appear before
         God now on our behalf" (Heb. 9:24).
         (b.) "By one offering he has forever perfected those
         who are being sanctified. . . . Let us draw near in
         utter sincerity and absolute confidence, our hearts
         sprinkled clean from the evil which lay on our con-
         science" (Heb. 10:14, 22).
B. As citizens of the kingdom of God we praise Christ the King.
   1. We are citizens of the kingdom of God.
      a. We join the procession this morning.
         1.) We take the palm, sing the antiphons and psalms, re-
         cite the prayers, and walk in the procession.
         2.) Our participation in this ceremony is an expression of
         our faith in the victory of Christ.
      b. Our presence in this procession is an expression of our citi-
      zenship in the kingdom of God.
         1.) Willingly we join this procession as an expression of
         our desire to follow Christ.
         2.) We praise and glorify God for our redemption and for
         the gift of citizenship in his kingdom.
   2. We praise Christ by accepting the obligations of citizenship
   in his kingdom.
      a. Our praise of Christ does not end with this ceremony.
      b. Fulfilling the obligations of the kingdom of heaven is the

true praise of Christ.

1.) This is the following of Christ: the acceptance of the cross.

  (a.) "If any man wishes to come after me, he must deny his very self, take up his cross, and begin to follow in my footsteps" (Matt. 16:24).

  (b.) "May I never boast of anything but the cross of Our Lord Jesus Christ! Through it the world has been crucified to me and I to the world" (Gal. 6:14).

2.) To accept the cross of Christ in our lives is to praise him.

  (a.) The cross is the instrument of Christ's victory.

  (b.) Accepting the cross we honor and praise Christ as our salvation, resurrection, and life.

3.) In this way we present Christ to the world.

Conclusion: Our king brings us the security of his protection, the riches of his grace, the promise of his glory. "Blessed be he who comes as king in the name of the Lord!" (Luke 19:38).

PASSION SUNDAY
(Palm Sunday)

(After the reading of the Passion the priest may preach a homily.)

Introduction: Today as we begin Holy Week the Church turns our attention to the glorification of Christ through his passion and death. That Christ is glorified through his suffering is the theme of today's procession with the palms and the reading of the Passion.

The liturgy we celebrate today involves the life of each one of us. Through the liturgy we are reminded of our participation in the Paschal Mystery. Since we are to be glorified with Christ, St. Paul writes to us: "Your attitude must be Christ's" (Phil. 2:5).

I Christ is exalted because he rendered humble service to people.

  A. Christ is willing to render humble service to people.

    1. Christ willingly accepts humiliation.

      a. "Though he was in the form of God he did not deem equality with God something to be grasped at. Rather, he emptied himself and took the form of a slave, being born in the likeness of men" (Phil. 2:6,7).

    b. This text from St. Paul's Epistle to the Philippians refers to the Incarnation of Christ.

       1.) Christ is God and is entitled to all the divine privileges.

       2.) Christ is willing to humble himself in the Incarnation.

         (a.) Christ is always God, but he does not demand the glory and honor which are due him as God.

         (b.) Christ is a servant of humanity in his human nature.

2. Christ shows the degree of his humility in the obedient service he renders.

    a. Christ is an obedient servant who obeys the Will of the Father.

       1.) The heavenly Father decrees that we are redeemed by the obedience of Christ (cf. Rom. 5:19).

       2.) This obedience leads Christ to death on the cross, a form of execution meted out to slaves (cf. Phil. 2:8).

    b. Christ offers his life by dying on the cross to serve the needs of souls.

B. Christ is exalted in glory.

    1. Christ is exalted in the glory of the resurrection.

      a. "Because of this God highly exalted him and bestowed on him the name above every other name, so that at Jesus' name every knee must bend in the heavens, on the earth, and under the earth, and every tongue proclaim to the glory of God the Father: Jesus Christ is Lord" (Phil. 2:9-11).

      b. This text refers to Christ's glorification which begins in his resurrection.

        1.) In his resurrection Christ is glorified.

        2.) Because of the deep humility of Christ the heavenly Father gives him the highest glory.

        3.) In his resurrection Christ receives the name "Lord." The exaltation implied in this name is in contrast with the humiliation of Christ as a servant.

    2. Christ is exalted in the glory of heaven.

      a. Christ returns to his heavenly Father.

        1.) Christ mounts the heavenly throne.

        2.) Christ receives the acclamation of the universe which declares he is the Lord.

    b. The heavenly Father gives Christ the power to judge, to govern, and to save.
      1.) The entire universe pays tribute to Christ.
      2.) Human nature confesses its faith in the divinity of Christ.
      3.) Christ glorifies the Father with whom the salvation of the human race begins.

II Humility in the service of others assures one's glorification.
  A. Humility in the service of others is required.
    1. Humility is the foundation of service to one's neighbor.
      a. Humility is the recognition of the truth.
        1.) Humility recognizes the truth of God's sovereignty.
          (a.) God rules all creation and guides it to its perfection.
          (b.) To each individual God gives talents which should be used for the advancement of humanity.
        2.) Humility recognizes the truth of one's dependence upon God.
      b. Humility recognizes the role the individual plays in the Providence of God.
        1.) The humble person allows himself to be directed by God.
        2.) The humble soul always seeks to glorify God.
          (a.) The humble soul uses his talents for the purpose for which God gave them.
          (b.) The humble soul exercises his talents for the welfare of his neighbor.
          (c.) The humble soul does not seek his personal glory or undue praise.
    2. Humility enables one to be patient and kind as he serves his neighbor.
      a. Humility enables one to be patient as he serves his neighbor.
        1.) The humble person is patient as he faces the ignorance of some of the people he wants to help.
        2.) The humble person is patient as he tolerates the delays encountered when he tries to help others.
      b. Humility enables one to be kind as he serves his neighbor.
        1.) The humble person is gentle in his ministry to others and calm in all situations of life.

        2.) The humble soul is characterized by moderation in all
           his words and activities.

B. The humble person is glorified by God.

    1. In this life the humble soul is glorified by an increase of
      grace.

        a. The increase of grace perfects the work of the humble.

           1.) "But by God's favor I am what I am. This favor of his
              to me has not proved fruitless. Indeed, I have worked
              harder than all the others, not on my own but through
              the favor of God" (I Cor. 15:10).

           2.) "He said to me, My grace is enough for you, for in
              weakness power reaches perfection. And so I willingly
              boast of my weaknesses instead, that the power of
              Christ may rest upon me" (II Cor. 12:9).

        b. The increase of grace fulfills the promise Christ makes:
          "For everyone who exalts himself shall be humbled while
          he who humbles himself shall be exalted" (Luke 18:14).

    2. With Christ the humble soul is glorified in heaven.

        a. Sharing with Christ the humiliations of his life, the humble
          soul is united with Christ in glory (cf. Rom. 8:30; Phil.
          3:21).

        b. The humble soul who is with Christ in heaven sings the
          eternal song of the heavenly Father's holiness and love
          (cf. Apoc. 4:8-11; 5:11-14).

Conclusion: Like Christ the humble soul empties himself. The
emptying is the humiliation of self, motivated by a Christlike love.
With Christ the humble person gives glory to God in the service of
others. With Christ the humble person is glorified. "Your attitude
must be that of Christ" (Phil. 2:5).

MONDAY OF HOLY WEEK

Introduction: Yesterday, Palm Sunday, we celebrated the death
and the glorification of Christ in the Liturgy of the Procession of the
Palms and in the reading of the Passion of Our Lord. Today, to pro-
long the effect of this celebration on our lives, the Church asks us to
pray the Responsorial Psalm, a prayer of confidence.

    This prayer and its sentiment of confidence also prepare us for
the celebration of the great mysteries later this week when the

liturgy will remind us that we are to work out our salvation. This is
not a cheerless task. The Responsorial Psalm for today reminds us
that we can confidently expect to enjoy the fruit of the redemption
wrought by Christ.

I Faith reveals that God is light and salvation.
   A. Faith is a gift from God whereby a person trusts God and ac-
      cepts his Word.
      1. Faith is a gift from God.
         a. God always takes the initiative, giving all that is required
           for salvation.
         b. Faith is freely given by God in order that individuals may
           know him and come to salvation.
      2. By faith a person trusts God and accepts his Word.
         a. "Faith" is the translation of an Old Testament word that
           means "to be firm or solid" or "to be true."
           1.) God is worthy of belief because he is true and faithful
             to his word.
           2.) God does not speak falsely nor does he change his
             mind (cf. Num. 23:19).
           3.) "The word of our God stands forever" (Isa. 40:8).
         b. Because of this quality of fidelity, God is the worthy re-
           cipient of our confidence and the source of security for all
           people.
   B. The psalmist is confirmed in his belief that God is light and sal-
      vation.
      1. The psalmist believes that God is light and salvation.
         a. The psalmist believes that God is light.
           1.) God is a guiding presence in the life of the psalmist.
             (a.) God illuminates the path of the psalmist (cf. Ps.
                18:29).
             (b.) God opens the eyes of the psalmist that he "may
                not sleep in death" and that he may "gaze upon the
                loveliness of the Lord . . ." (Ps. 13:4; Ps. 27:4).
           2.) As the sunlight gives joy to human hearts so is God, the
             light, a source of happiness for the psalmist.
         b. The psalmist believes that God is the source of salvation.
           1.) In the Old Testament the word "salvation" signifies "to
             be taken out of a dangerous situation."
           2.) When certain evildoers attack the psalmist God pro-
             tects and frees him from danger (cf. Ps. 27:2, 5-6).

2. Experience confirms the psalmist in his faith.
   a. The faith of the psalmist is confirmed by the national experience of Israel.
      1.) The history of Israel confirms the faith of the psalmist in the saving power of God.
         (a.) In times of national trials God controls the events by which the Israelites are saved.
         (b.) God raises up individuals to lead the Israelites to safety.
      2.) Throughout history God has always saved those Israelites who hoped in him.
   b. The faith of the psalmist is confirmed by his personal experience.
      1.) The psalmist is saved when he cries out to God, seeking the divine help.
      2.) The psalmist says God illumines his life, filling it with happiness.

II We have confidence in Christ who is our light and our salvation.
   A. Faith reveals that Christ is our light and our salvation.
      1. Faith reveals that Christ is our light.
         a. Sacred Scripture, a font of faith, reveals Christ as the light of the world.
            1.) As the Servant of Yahweh who is the light of the world, Christ fulfills the prophecy of the Old Testament (cf. Isa. 42:6; 49:6).
            2.) Christ is the light of the world.
               (a.) "Whatever came to be in him, found life, life for the light of men" (John 1:4).
               (b.) "I am the light of the world. No follower of mine shall ever walk in darkness; no, he shall possess the light of life" (John 8:12).
         b. Christ enlightens everyone by his law of charity.
            1.) "He who obeys the commandments he has from me is the man who loves me; and he who loves me will be loved by my Father. I too will love him and reveal myself to him" (John 14:21).
            2.) "As the Father has loved me, so I have loved you. Live on in my love" (John 15:9).
            3.) "This is my commandment: Love one another as I have loved you . . . You are my friends if you do what I

command you" (John 15:12, 14).
2. Faith reveals that Christ is our salvation.
   a. Faith reveals that the Father sends us his Son to be the source of our salvation.
      1.) God makes known to us his desire for our holiness through faith.
      2.) "God chose us in him before the world began, to be holy and blameless in his sight, to be full of love; he likewise predestined us through Christ Jesus to be his adopted sons—such was his will and pleasure—that all might praise the glorious favor he has bestowed on us in his beloved" (Eph. 1:4-6).
         (a.) God designates Christ to achieve our salvation by his redemptive action.
         (b.) We conform to the plan for our salvation to the degree by which we conform to Christ through whom we become the adopted children of God.
         (c.) As adopted children of God we achieve our salvation.
   b. Christ is very conscious of his role as the savior of the human race.
      1.) "Yes, God so loved the world that he gave his only Son, that whoever believes in him may not die but may have eternal life" (John 3:16).
      2.) ". . . no one comes to the Father but through me" (John 14:6).
      3.) Christ reminds us that he must be lifted up so that he may draw all hearts to himself, and that those who look upon him so lifted up may have eternal life (cf. John 3:14,15; John 12:32).
B. We place our trust in Christ, our light and our salvation.
   1. We place our faith in Christ our light.
      a. We are the children of light (cf. John 3:19; John 12:36).
         1.) We "walk in the light" to remain in union with Christ.
         2.) Because we do not hide in darkness, our actions are seen by all people for the glory of God (cf. John 1:50).
      b. Christ changes our lives: "You, however, are a chosen race, a royal priesthood, a holy nation, a people he claims for his own to proclaim the glorious works of the One who called you from the darkness into his marvelous light" (I Peter 2:9).

      1.) Christ takes us from the darkness of sin that we may share the brilliant light of God.

      2.) We hope for a transformation into the beauty of eternal life.

          (a.) In heaven we shall reflect the splendor of God (Apoc. 21:23 ff.).

          (b.) In heaven we shall be illuminated by contemplating the face of God (cf. Apoc. 22:4-5).

  2. We place our faith in Christ our salvation.

    a. Our salvation is accomplished by Christ.

      1.) "Now that we have been justified by faith, we are at peace with God through our Lord Jesus Christ" (Rom. 5:1).

      2.) Christ reconciles us with God through his death and resurrection.

          (a.) We are redeemed by Christ.

          (b.) The merits of Christ, given to us by the mercy of God, bestow on us a sense of security as we strive for salvation.

    b. We strive for salvation, confident of the merits of Christ.

      1.) At the end of time we shall receive the perfect enjoyment of our salvation in the happiness of heaven.

      2.) Each passing day brings us closer to the glory of heaven as the merits of Christ are applied to our souls through our prayers, reception of the sacraments, and good works.

Conclusion: We look forward to the great celebration at the end of this week; Easter reminds us of our victory. Christ is our light and our salvation!

TUESDAY OF HOLY WEEK

Introduction: Commentators agree that the Responsorial Psalm is the prayer of an old man who suffers from the attacks of his enemies. This unknown psalmist writes of his full life. He suffers but is not defeated. His experience with life does not destroy him. The psalm he has composed is a prayer which proves that the mercy of God "is from age to age on those who fear him" (Luke 1:50).

I The psalmist expresses his reverential fear of God.
  A. Reverential fear of God originates in faith.
    1. Reverential fear of God is respect for God which is born of
       faith.
       a. God does not terrify a soul to whom he reveals himself.
          1.) The Lord says to Gideon: "Be calm, do not fear. You
              shall not die" (Judg. 6:22-23).
          2.) "Fear not, Daniel, he continued; from the first day you
              made up your mind to acquire understanding and
              humble yourself before God . . ." (Dan. 10:12).
          3.) Our Lord frequently uses the phrase, "Fear not" when
              he reveals himself to the Apostles.
       b. Reverential fear, respect for God, prompts one to accept
          God's Will and to avoid offending God because of respect
          for him who is a loving Father.
    2. Reverential fear, respect for God, is the expression of one's
       belief in the majesty, the goodness, the justice, and the mer-
       cy of God.
       a. Respect for God is expressed by humility as one stands be-
          fore him.
       b. Confidence also expresses one's respect for the goodness
          and mercy of God.
  B. The soul of the psalmist is filled with reverential fear of God.
    1. The psalmist prays that he will remain united to God.
       a. The psalmist places his trust in God in a time of distress.
          1.) "In you, O Lord, I take refuge. . . . Be my rock of ref-
              uge, a stronghold to give me safety, for you are my
              rock and my fortress" (Ps. 71:1-3).
          2.) "On you I depend from my birth; from my mother's
              womb you are my strength; constant has been my
              hope in you" (Ps. 71:6).
       b. The psalmist declares his dependence upon God.
          1.) "For you are my hope, O Lord; my trust, O God, from
              my youth" (Ps. 71:5).
          2.) "Cast me not off in my old age; as my strength fails,
              forsake me not" (Ps. 71:9).
    2. The psalmist dedicates himself to proclaim the goodness of
       God.
       a. The psalmist wants other people to love God and to re-
          spect his holiness.
       b. His experience of God's goodness fills the soul of the

psalmist, and he wishes to share this with future generations.

  1.) "I will treat of the mighty works of the Lord: O God, I
      will tell of your singular justice" (Ps. 71:16).
  2.) "And now that I am old and gray, O God, forsake me
      not till I proclaim your strength to every generation
      that is to come. . . . My lips shall shout for joy as I sing
      your praises" (Ps. 71:18,23).

II We express our reverential fear of God.
  A. In the liturgy we celebrate the greatness of God with respect.
    1. In the liturgy we celebrate the greatness of God.
       a. The prayers and the readings of the Mass remind us of the
          power of God as they remind us of the great works of
          God: creation and redemption.
       b. The mercy of God motivates our participation in the Mass
          and our personal prayers.
    2. We show our respect for God in the celebration of the litur-
       gy.
       a. Respectfully we listen to the Word of God and apply the
          lessons of the Mass to our daily lives.
       b. As we celebrate the liturgy we stand and kneel to show
          our respect for the divine goodness, power, mercy, and
          love.
  B. Respect for God is our motive for keeping the commandments.
    1. We do not consider God a stern judge, but a Father who
       loves us.
       a. We are aware that we are the children of God.
       b. We respect God as a child respects his parent.
          1.) We have a filial attachment to God which is shown by
              our love for him and our obedience to him.
          2.) It is this filial attachment to God that strengthens us in
              time of temptation and helps us to keep the command-
              ments.
    2. Our respect for God enables us to reveal the image of God to
       others as we keep the commandments.
       a. As we keep the commandments that protect the rights of
          our neighbors, we reflect the justice of God.
       b. As we observe the law of charity by our acts of kindness,
          we reflect the goodness and mercy of God in our lives.

Conclusion: The filial fear of God, of which the psalmist wrote, is a characteristic of the religious person. Flowing from a lively faith, reverential fear of God leads a soul into the mystery of Christ and to the true experience of God which is the purpose of our lives.

WEDNESDAY OF HOLY WEEK

Introduction: The liturgy for today fixes our attention on the virtue of loyalty to God. In the Mass we celebrate the loyalty of Christ to the Will of the heavenly Father. In the next few days, as we celebrate the great mystery of redemption, the fidelity of Christ to the Father is the center of our attention.

The Responsorial Psalm for today's Mass is the prayer of a persecuted man who, like Christ, suffers because of his loyalty to God. The psalmist, like Christ, is not defeated. Like Christ, the psalmist is pursued by relentless enemies and held in contempt by his neighbors.

I The liturgy for this week teaches us loyalty to God.
  A. The psalmist, in all the circumstances of his life, is faithful to God.
    1. The psalmist is loyal to God.
      a. The psalmist imitates the fidelity that God shows to Israel.
      b. The psalmist finds strength to remain loyal to God in prayer.
    2. In all his trials the psalmist remains loyal to God.
      a. Laboring under a false accusation, the psalmist is loyal to God.
        1.) The psalmist is charged with a crime of injustice: "Too many for my strength are they who wrongfully are my enemies. Must I restore what I did not steal?" (Ps. 69:5).
        2.) Under this false accusation by his enemies, the psalmist prays to God (cf. Ps. 69:2,14).
      b. His fellow citizens mock the piety of the psalmist, but he remains faithful to God.
        1.) The psalmist is very sensitive to the insults and rejection he endures because of his faith (cf. Ps. 69:9,13).
        2.) The psalmist describes the physical effect of his intense, prolonged prayers: "I am wearied with calling, my throat is parched . . ." (Ps. 69:4).

      c. The psalmist also suffers because he is zealous for the house of God (cf. Ps. 69:10).
- **B.** Christ gives us an example of loyalty to God.
  - 1. The liturgy of these final days of Holy Week celebrates the loyalty of Christ to his heavenly Father.
    - a. The liturgy of Holy Week celebrates the passion, death, and resurrection of Christ.
    - b. The loyalty of Christ to the Will of his heavenly Father sustains him in his suffering and is the reason for his glorification in the resurrection.
  - 2. The loyalty of Christ is the perfect worship of the heavenly Father and leads to our sanctification.
    - a. The loyalty of Christ is the perfect worship of the heavenly Father.
      - 1.) Christ is the loyal high priest who offers the perfect sacrifice to his heavenly Father.
        - (a.) Christ offers himself as the most perfect gift to his heavenly Father.
        - (b.) Christ offers his sacrifice with perfect conformity of his will to the Will of the Father.
      - 2.) Because of his perfect loyalty to his heavenly Father, Christ's sacrifice is accepted and his prayer is heard by the Father.
    - b. The loyalty of Christ to the Father leads to our sanctification.
      - 1.) Christ is loyal to the plan devised by God for the salvation of the human race.
        - (a.) Persecuted by the elders of the people and by the Roman soldiers, Christ does not abandon the work of salvation.
        - (b.) Dying on the cross, Christ does not come down from it but remains on the cross to complete the work of redemption.
      - 2.) Loyal to the Father, Christ fulfills all the prophecies, prays for the forgiveness of his enemies, and dies for our salvation.

II We are inspired to remain loyal to God.
- **A.** We are loyal to God in the actions of daily life.
  - 1. Loyalty is a very common description of the followers of Christ.

      a. "Live according to what you have learned and accepted, what you have heard me say and seen me do. Then will the God of peace be with you" (Phil. 4:9).

      b. St. Paul instructs the people of Philippi to live according to the faith they have received, i.e., to be loyal and faithful to the teaching of Our Lord.

   2. Our loyalty to Christ is shown by the way we live.

      a. We are loyal to Christ as we faithfully observe his law of justice, love, and mercy toward our neighbor.

      b. Loyalty to Christ is characteristic of a life directed by the Holy Spirit.

      c. Our loyalty to Christ appears in all the details of our daily life, for as Christ says: "If you can trust a man in little things, you can also trust him in greater" (Luke 16:10).

B. Loyalty, which is the soul of the liturgy—the new covenant we live—assures us of salvation.

   1. Celebrating the Last Supper, the new covenant, Christ teaches us how to adhere to its terms in our lives.

      a. "Live on in my love. You will live in my love if you keep my commandments, even as I have kept my Father's commandments and live in his love" (John 15:10).

      b. "Your business is to follow me" (John 21:22).

         1.) Christ directs us to be loyal to the obligations of fraternal charity.

         2.) Christ gives us "examples" of fraternal charity at the Last Supper.

           (a.) Christ washes the feet of the Apostles.

           (b.) Christ gives us the command to be loyal to his law of charity.

           (c.) Christ gives us the Holy Eucharist, the new covenant, that we may be loyal to this covenant of love.

   2. We are assured of our resurrection by loyalty to the new covenant, our liturgy.

      a. The new covenant of fraternal charity makes demands of us.

         1.) It requires that we struggle to avoid offenses against charity.

         2.) It requires that we be vigilant and prayerful so as to remain loyal to the words of Christ (cf. Matt. 6:13; Matt. 26:41).

      b. Loyalty to Christ's covenant with us assures our resurrection.

1.) God rewards the effort we make: "The God of all grace, who called you to his everlasting glory in Christ, will himself restore, confirm, strengthen, and establish those who have suffered a little while" (I Peter 5:10).
2.) Christ asks our continued loyalty that he may share his eternal life with us.
    (a.) "All this I tell you that my joy may be yours and your joy may be complete" (John 15:11).
    (b.) "His master said to him, well done! You are an industrious and reliable servant. Since you were dependable in a small matter I will put you in charge of larger affairs. Come share your master's joy"! (Matt. 25:21).

Conclusion: In the Old Testament God requires fidelity to the covenant (Joshua 24:14). The psalmist and Christ exemplify this loyalty to God in all the events of their lives. We follow that example. We are loyal to God who invites us: "Come share your master's joy" (Matt. 25:21).

HOLY THURSDAY

Introduction: The Responsorial Psalm for today's Mass is a prayer of thanksgiving. Like you the psalmist comes to the Temple to pay his vow and to offer God a sacrifice of thanksgiving.

We do not know the name of the psalmist or anything about his life. He may have been, like you, a farmer, a merchant, a doctor, a lawyer, or a blue-collar worker. Like you the psalmist has a reason to go to the Temple: He wants to thank God.

I The psalmist expresses his gratitude to God.
  A. God healed the psalmist.
    1. We do not know the nature of the illness that tormented the psalmist.
    2. The psalmist acknowledges God's merciful healing.
      a. Medical science, as we know it, did not exist at the time this psalm was written.
      b. The psalmist acknowledges the compassion of God (cf. Ps. 116:2).
        1.) God alone is responsible for curing the psalmist.

      2.) The psalmist expresses his dependence on God for the cure received and for the protection God gives him.

B. The psalmist pays his vow to thank Almighty God.

  1. At the Temple, before all the people, the psalmist acknowledges an indebtedness to God.

    a. Fulfilling his vow, the psalmist declares that God has rescued him from a much-dreaded fate.

    b. The psalmist offers to God the drink offering which he refers to as the "cup of salvation."

  2. The gratitude expressed in this psalm must flow from an intense religious experience of the psalmist.

    a. In his prayer of thanksgiving the psalmist expresses his past, as well as his present and future, dependence on God.

    b. His sense of gratitude motivates the psalmist to rededicate himself to the service of God.

II We offer to God the sacrifice of thanksgiving.

  A. We thank God for his mercy.

    1. The mercy of God cures our sinfulness.

      a. Through the passion, death, and resurrection of Christ our sins are forgiven.

      b. The mercy of God protects us from future evil.

        1.) Through the merits of Christ, which are applied to our souls through the sacraments and prayer, one gains control of his passions.

        2.) The grace of God keeps us alert to occasions of sin and aware of opportunities to practice virtue.

    2. We are grateful to God.

      a. We wish to express the gratitude that fills our hearts.

        1.) Publicly we acknowledge our debt to God for his many gifts of grace.

          (a.) We are grateful to God for the grace by which he adopts us as his children.

          (b.) We admit that God is good and merciful to us, for he forgives our offenses.

        2.) We seek ways by which we can express our gratitude.

          (a.) We offer to God our prayers in the spirit of gratitude.

          (b.) We make promises to God, offering our actions as a thanksgiving to him.

   b. Although our hearts are filled with gratitude it seems we
      cannot express adequately our appreciation for all God
      does for us.
      1.) We are aware of our limitations.
      2.) The goodness of God toward us is overwhelming.
B. We offer the Mass as our thanksgiving to God.
   1. The Mass is the greatest act of thanksgiving we can offer to
      God.
      a. The Mass continues the thanksgiving Christ offered to the
         heavenly Father.
         1.) The Mass continues the experience of Christ's grati-
             tude.
             (a.) Before Our Lord consecrates the bread and wine
                  at the Last Supper he thanks the heavenly Father
                  (cf. Matt. 26:27; Mark 14:23; Luke 22:17,19).
             (b.) Before the consecration in the Mass the priest ex-
                  presses the thanksgiving of the Church to the heav-
                  enly Father (cf. words of the Prefaces for the
                  Mass).
         2.) It is through Christ that we receive every grace from
             the Father, and it is through Christ that we offer our
             gratitude to the Father.
      b. The thanksgiving of the Mass is of infinite value.
         1.) This is the adequate gratitude offered to the heavenly
             Father.
         2.) The value of the Mass is derived from the excellence of
             Christ, the priest and the victim of this sacrifice.
   2. We unite ourselves to Christ, the priest and the victim of
      this sacrifice.
      a. We unite our intention with that of Christ as we thank the
         Father for his gifts.
      b. As the priest prepares the chalice for the offertory of the
         Mass, he mingles a little water with the wine; this action
         symbolizes our union with Christ.

Conclusion: We, like the psalmist, are aware of the debt of gratitude
we owe to God. Like the psalmist we ask: "How shall I make a return to the Lord for all the good he has done for me?" (Ps. 116:12).
And like the psalmist we answer our question: "The cup of salvation
I will take up, and I will call upon the name of the Lord" (Ps.
116:13). Our cup of salvation is the Mass.

GOOD FRIDAY

(After the reading of The Passion it is suggested
that the priest preach a homily.)

Introduction: The liturgy for today focuses our attention on the crucifixion of Christ. This is the center of human history; it is the moment of human redemption. Dying on the cross, Christ fulfills all the Promises and prophecies by which God prepared the world for redemption. Since the moment of Christ's death all the events of world history can be read as the human acceptance or rejection of that salvific event. Today we gather in this church to celebrate in a sacramental way the redemptive action of Christ. The components of this celebration, namely, The Liturgy of the Word, The Veneration of the Cross, The Reception of Holy Communion, fix in our mind the truth that Christ offers himself for us and stimulates our hearts to approach him with loving confidence.

I Christ is the eternal priest.
  A. Christ is a priest.
    1. Christ is declared a priest by the heavenly Father.
        a. "The Lord has sworn, and he will not repent: you are a priest forever, according to the order of Melchizedek" (Ps. 110:4).
        b. The excellence of the priesthood is indicated by the words "according to the order of Melchizedek."
            1.) Melchizedek was a prophetic type which Christ fulfilled.
            2.) Both Melchizedek and Christ were kings as well as priests; both offered bread and wine; both received their priesthood from God and not through descent from Levi (cf. Gen. 14:18; Heb. 7).
    2. Christ fulfilled the functions of a priest.
        a. In the Old Testament, priests served the Law.
            1.) Christ served the Law by bringing it to perfection (Matt. 5:17f.).
            2.) Christ was not bound by the letter of the Law, but he explained and exemplified its spirit (Matt. 5:20-48).
            3.) During his life and at the time of his death on the cross, Christ exposed the meaning of the first and greatest

commandment and of the second commandment,
which is like the first (Matt. 22:34-40).

   b. Christ is a priest-mediator.

      1.) The role of a priest as mediator is to offer to God the
offerings of the people and to bestow on the people
the gifts and blessings of God.

      2.) Christ by his fidelity offered the heavenly Father the
purest worship and gained for the human race the gift
of redemption.

B. Christ offered the sacrifice of Calvary.

  1. Christ spoke of his sacrifice in the priestly terms of the Old
Testament.

    a. Christ referred to his death as a sacrifice of expiation:
"The Son of Man has not come to be served but to serve—
to give his life in ransom for the many" (Mark 10:45).

    b. Christ said his was a sacrifice of the covenant. "He said to
them: This is my blood of the covenant, to be poured out
on behalf of many" (Mark 14:24).

    c. Frequently Christ associated his death with the sacrifice
of the Paschal Lamb.

  2. Christ the priest offered himself as the victim of the sacrifice
of Calvary.

    a. Christ offered the Father the clean oblation, the perfect
sacrifice (cf. Mal. 1:11).

      1.) Christ offered the Father the most perfect victim in
sacrifice—himself.

      2.) Christ offered himself to the Father with the most per-
fect intentions.

    b. The sacrifice of Christ is a new covenant by which God is
glorified and the sins of men are expiated.

C. The priesthood of Christ is eternal.

  1. Christ ascended into heaven.

    a. "In the days when he was in the flesh he offered prayers
and supplications with loud cries and tears to God, who
was able to save him from death, and he was heard because of his reverence . . . and when perfected, he became
the source of eternal salvation for all who obey him"
(Heb. 5:7,9).

      1.) These words refer not only to the passion and death of
Christ, but also to his glorification.

      2.) God delivers Christ from the grip of death, i.e., he

does not experience corruption; he rises from the tomb and is glorified before the throne of God.
   b. "But when Christ came as high priest of the good things which have come to be, he entered once for all into the sanctuary, passing through the greater and more perfect tabernacle not made with hands, that is, not belonging to this creation" (Heb. 9:11).
      1.) Unlike the high priest of the Old Law who entered the Holy of Holies only once a year, Christ entered heaven after he offered his sacrifice, and he remains there.
      2.) Christ is the perfect cause of the salvation of the human race.
   2. In the glory of heaven Christ continues to intercede for us.
      a. "We have such a high priest, who has taken his seat at the right hand of the throne of the Majesty in heaven.... Now every high priest is appointed to offer gifts and sacrifices; hence the necessity for this one to have something to offer" (Heb. 8:1-3).
         1.) Christ in heaven presents the merits of the sacrifice of Calvary to the heavenly Father.
         2.) In heaven Christ presents his glorified humanity to the Father.
            (a.) His soul manifests to the Father Our Lord's desire to adore and to thank the Father.
            (b.) Christ communicates to us the graces he merited for us on Calvary.
      b. "Jesus, because he remains forever, has a priesthood which does not pass away. Therefore he is always able to save those who approach God through him, since he forever lives to make intercession for them" (Heb. 7:24-25).

II We approach Christ with confidence.
   A. Christ is like us in everything except sin.
      1. "For we do not have a high priest who is unable to sympathize with our weakness, but one who was tempted in every way that we are, yet never sinned" (Heb. 4:15).
         a. Christ our high priest is true man; he is chosen from among men to be a priest.
         b. Christ succeeded in rejecting temptation.
            1.) At the beginning of his public life Christ was tempted by the devil.

      2.) In the Garden of Olives Christ was tempted to put aside the work of redemption.

   2. Christ did not sin.

     a. Christ endured very intense temptation, but he did not sin.

     b. To sin means that one fails to bear the temptation and succumbs to it.

 B. Christ is best qualified to help us.

   1. Christ is identified with the people he serves.

     a. Like many human beings Christ learned obedience by his sufferings (cf. Heb. 5:8).

     b. In a very human way Christ prayed in the time of temptation to gain control of his human emotions (cf. Heb. 5:7).

   2. Christ sympathizes with us.

     a. Christ knows by experience, his suffering, what obstacles must be overcome before a person can obey God.

     b. Christ conquers sin and temptation, and is best able to help us.

Conclusion: Today, celebrating the sacred liturgy, we recall the death of Christ on the cross. Christ passes through the humiliating experience of crucifixion. From this experience Christ passes into the heavens (Heb. 4:14). We hold fast to our profession of faith in his merits (cf. Heb. 4:14). "Let us confidently approach the throne of grace to receive mercy and favor and to find help in the time of need" (Heb. 4:16).

MEDITATIONS ON THE SEVEN LAST WORDS

The former celebration of the Seven Last Words on Good Friday is not an integral part of the liturgy for today. However, in certain areas permission has been granted for the celebration of "The Three Hours." The following considerations are offered to assist those souls who participate in this ceremony. Also it is hoped that any individual who may be prompted by his private devotion to meditate on the death of Christ may find in these outlines a stimulus for prayer.

THE FIRST WORD

Introduction: While the soldiers were crucifying Christ, Pilate's ironical attitude toward the Jewish leaders became evident. Pilate had asked the priests what crime Christ had committed and if they desired the crucifixion of their king. Then he had nailed above the head of Christ a placard which he, Pilate, wrote and which announced: "This is the King of the Jews" (Luke 23:38). The placard was written in the language of the country, Hebrew; in the language of the government, Latin; and in the language of the educated, Greek. Seeing this sign, the high priest recognized the implied insult. The leaders of the people tried to have the sign removed, but Pilate refused. Thus Christ died as a king, and on the cross he showed the magnanimity of a king.

I Christ, dying on the cross, was magnanimous.
   A. Magnanimity is greatness of soul.
      1. When one uses the small or ordinary things of life in the best possible way, one is exercising greatness of soul.
      2. When an individual puts the best things to the best use, he is exercising greatness of soul.
      3. Magnanimity is associated with the virtue of fortitude.
         a. Determination—firmness of mind—is required by the individual who attempts to accomplish difficult things.
         b. Firmness of mind is difficult to maintain in the face of death.
   B. In the moment of death Christ was magnanimous.
      1. Christ made the best use of the greatest natural gift he possessed, his life.
         a. Christ offered his life to God the Father to honor him in reparation for the sin of man.
         b. Christ offered his life for the welfare of each individual.
      2. Christ was determined to accomplish what was good.
         a. With courage Christ remained on the cross.
         b. Insulted, Christ did not change his mind.
            1.) "Save yourself now by coming down from the cross" (Mark 15:30).
            2.) "He saved others; let him save himself if he is the Messiah of God, the chosen one" (Luke 23:35).

II The virtue of magnanimity is needed by each one of us.

    A. We have been called by God to accomplish great things.

        1. By reason of our baptism we have been called by God to imitate Christ.

            a. To accomplish this we must make the best possible use of our lives.

                1.) We must strive to live each day according to our vocation.

                    (a.) Our vocation has its own grace which conforms us to Christ.

                    (b.) We follow this advice: "Do not neglect the gift you received . . . attend to your duties" (I Tim. 4:14-15).

                2.) We must make the best possible use of the ordinary things of life.

                    (a.) We consecrate time by our attendance at Mass and by our personal prayer.

                    (b.) The routine tasks of a day we offer to God for the spiritual and temporal welfare of the Church, for our country, and for our families and friends.

            b. We identify ourselves with Christ.

                1.) Doctors and nurses see themselves doing the work of Christ as they heal the blind, the lame, and those "with a variety of diseases" (cf. Luke 4:40).

                2.) A teacher, a laborer, or even a child can find in his life many parallels with the life and actions of Our Lord.

        2. We have been called by God to contribute to the spiritual welfare of all men.

            a. We can exclaim with St. Paul: "I have been crucified with Christ" (Gal. 2:19).

            b. We experience pain and suffering, sorrow and disappointment; we offer these to God, in union with the sufferings of Christ, in reparation for sin.

    B. We live magnanimously because of Christ.

        1. Our greatness of soul is founded on hope.

            a. We do not intend to accomplish everything by ourselves.

                1.) We know our limitations, and we admit that "God chose those whom the world considers absurd to shame the wise; he singled out the weak of this world to shame the strong" (I Cor. 1:27).

                2.) Like Paul we can say we go about our tasks in fear and trepidation (cf. I Cor. 2:3).

      b. Our success, we are certain, rests on the power of God (cf. I Cor. 2:5).
          1.) The death of Christ is the source of the strength by which we can conquer all obstacles.
          2.) We hope in the mercy of God which is given to us by the death of Christ.
   2. Our greatness of soul is marked by courage.
      a. Nothing will prevent us from reaching our goals.
          1.) We do not say this as an empty boast.
          2.) We say it because we are confident of God's help.
      b. The example of Christ sustains us.
          1.) In pain and suffering on the cross Christ prayed that we would be forgiven and strengthened by his grace.
          2.) In rising from the tomb Christ prayed: "Peace be with you . . . men's sins are forgiven them" (John 20:23).

Conclusion: The hardships we endure and the temptations we experience do not distract us from our purpose. Christ prayed for us. By that prayer we are saved.

THE SECOND WORD

Introduction: The soldiers finished the task of crucifixion. They began to divide the garments of the cricified. Unknowingly they fulfilled the prophecy: "They divided my garments among them and for my vesture they cast lots" (Ps. 22:19). Then the soldiers rolled dice for the seamless robe of Christ. After their game was over they stood up and took their positions as the guards of those condemned to die. Although this indifference is revolting we realize that one of the thieves eventually opened his heart and was forgiven.

I Each person is free to open his heart to God's mercy or to keep it closed.
  A. God does not force a person to open his heart.
    1. God is always willing to give his grace.
      a. God sent his Son to redeem us.
      b. God always makes grace available to all men.
    2. The scene of the crucifixion impresses us with the freedom of the human will.
      a. There were many who refused to open their hearts to

God's mercy.

1.) The Roman soldiers were indifferent to the crucifixion.

   (a.) They had just nailed Christ and two thieves to
crosses.

   (b.) Indifferent about what they had done, the soldiers
ate their noonday meal and then began to roll dice
for the garments of the dying.

2.) Some of the crowd around the cross continued to
mock Christ.

   (a.) "People going by kept insulting him, tossing their
heads and saying, 'Ha, ha! So you were going to
destroy the temple and rebuild it in three days' "
(Mark 15:29).

   (b.) "The chief priest and the scribes also joined in and
jeered: 'He saved others but he cannot save himself' " (Mark 15:31).

b. The Gospels tell us that both of the thieves crucified with
Christ joined with the others in mocking him.

1.) "The men who had been crucified with him likewise
kept taunting him" (Mark 15:32).

2.) "The insurgents who had been crucified with him kept
taunting him in the same way" (Matt. 27:44).

B. One of the thieves opened his heart to God's mercy.

1. Here we face a great mystery.

a. We do not know what happened in the depths of the Good
Thief's soul.

b. This is a mystery of grace and of one man's willingness to
accept God's mercy.

2. Insofar as we can judge we say the Good Thief accepted the
forgiveness offered by Christ.

a. This man heard Our Lord speak the first word from the
cross, which was one of forgiveness.

b. The Good Thief accepted this gift of God.

1.) His soul was touched by God's grace, and he stopped
insulting Christ.

2.) In the moment of his conversion the Good Thief tried
to influence his companion: "Have you no fear of God,
seeing you are under the same sentence? We deserve
it, after all. We are only paying the price for what
we've done, but this man has done nothing wrong"

(Luke 23:40-41).
3.) Then this dying man spoke to Christ.
   (a.) "He then said, 'Jesus, remember me when you enter upon your reign' " (Luke 23:42).
   (b.) "And Jesus replied, 'I assure you: this day you will be with me in paradise' " (Luke 23:43).

II We can apply this lesson to our lives.
  A. It is possible for us to leave today's service indifferent to grace.
    1. We cannot blame the Roman soldiers or members of the crowd who were present at the crucifixion.
      a. Like the Roman soldiers we can play our own game with the grace of God.
        1.) There is some excuse for the conduct of the Roman soldiers, who acted in ignorance.
        2.) In a spiritual sense we can roll dice by gambling away the occasion of grace, delaying our prayers, or toying with temptation.
      b. Like some of the Jewish leaders we can insult Christ.
        1.) We can refuse the inspirations of prayer.
        2.) We can reject the actual grace that would help us to be kind and considerate toward others.
    2. We must decide how we shall celebrate the death of Christ.
      a. We cannot expect that our presence here will automatically produce a change of heart.
        1.) Presence at the scene of our redemption did not automatically change the hearts of some people.
        2.) The grace of God requires our cooperation.
      b. In the celebration of our redemption we can dispose ourselves for God's mercy.
        1.) All of today's ceremonies remind us of our salvation.
        2.) We celebrate this mystery with faith, aware of our need for grace.
  B. Today's ceremonies help to open our hearts to the mercy of God.
    1. We pray for the graces we need.
    2. We are confident that God's mercy is granted to us.
      a. Like the Good Thief we can gain paradise.
      b. We open our hearts to God.
        1.) We live by faith in the mercy of God.
        2.) We live by hope in the power of God.

3.) We live by love for the God who loved us so much that
he sent us his Son.

   (a.) We live in the fear of God, respecting him.

   (b.) We live in a spirit of piety, aware that our Father
will call us home.

Conclusion: "This day you will be with me in paradise" (Luke
23:43).

THE THIRD WORD

Introduction: We read in the Gospel of St. John: "Near the cross of
Jesus there stood his mother ..." (John 19:25). Although the Romans
usually kept people away from the crucified, there were occasions
when close relatives of a dying man were permitted near his cross.
No doubt the Roman soldiers thought that Mary, John, Mary the
wife of Clopas, and Mary Magdalene would not disturb the dying,
and so they were permitted to stand near Christ.

I Mary was near her children on Calvary.

  A. Mary was near Christ on Calvary.

    1. Mary had offered Christ to God the Father and had then pre-
sented her son to men.

      a. Our Lord was an infant when Mary offered him to God
and presented him to men.

        1.) When Mary took Christ to Jerusalem for the rite of cir-
cumcision she offered him to God the Father (cf. Luke
2:22f.).

        2.) Mary presented Christ to Simeon and Anna (cf. Luke
2:25ff.).

      b. When Christ was twelve years old Mary took him to Jeru-
salem (cf. Luke 2:41ff.).

        1.) There Christ assumed the obligations of the Law of
Moses.

        2.) While in the Temple Our Lord instructed the learned
doctors of the Law.

    2. On Calvary Mary offered Christ to the heavenly Father and
presented him to men.

      a. This was her perfect offering to God.

        1.) Christ, dying on the cross, was the perfect sacrifice to

God the Father.

 2.) Mary united herself in love and suffering with Christ as she accepted the Will of God manifested in the death of Christ.

 b. Mary offered Christ to the world.

  1.) She accepted the Will of God which decreed that Christ should die for all.

  2.) Mary never hesitated to present Christ to men.

   (a.) The shepherds and the Magi found Christ with his mother.

   (b.) Simeon and Anna could rest in peace because they saw the salvation of Israel in Mary's arms.

   (c.) The hour had come on Calvary for Mary to present the Savior of the world to mankind.

B. On Calvary Mary was near John.

 1. Christ committed the care of Mary to John.

  a. Looking down from the cross, Christ saw his suffering mother.

   1.) He knew she would be alone after his death because she had no other children.

   2.) Our Lord wanted to provide for Mary his mother.

    (a.) ". . . Jesus said to his mother, 'Woman, there is your son' " (John 19:26).

    (b.) "In turn he said to the disciple, 'There is your mother' " (John 19:27).

  b. John provided for Mary: "From that hour onward, the disciple took her into his care" (John 19:27).

 2. Mary accepted this exchange.

  a. On Calvary Mary accepted the son of Zebedee for the Son of God.

  b. Mary cared for John.

   1.) John provided the physical necessities of life for Mary.

   2.) Mary provided the spiritual insights that John needed for his life as an Apostle.

II Mary is near her children today.

 A. Mary is the spiritual mother of all men.

  1. It was on Calvary that Mary took upon herself the obligation of spiritual motherhood for all.

  2. It is through her that grace—supernatural life—comes to all.

   a. It is through Mary that grace—the supernatural life—is

distributed to all.
  b. It is through Mary that grace is distributed to nourish and
   protect the supernatural life in the souls of men.
B. With confidence we can pray to our mother.
  1. Like a mother, Mary is interested in her children.
   a. Mary is concerned about each one of us.
   b. Mary provides for us by her prayers before the throne of
    God.
  2. Mary provides us with insights into life.
   a. In times of doubt and questioning we may pray to Mary.
   b. She will provide the answers for us.

Conclusion: In a sacramental way we are present at Calvary today.
In faith we see the mystery of salvation, and we wish to enter it
deeply. Our Lord gives us the means to participate in this mystery
every day of our lives. Christ says to us: "There is your mother"
(John 19:27). Like John, we must from this moment onward take
her into our care with the assurance that she will take us into her
care.

THE FOURTH WORD

Introduction: St. Luke says: "It was now around midday, and darkness came over the whole land until midafternoon with an eclipse to
the sun" (Luke 23:44). Darkness is associated with what took place
as nature grieved over the death of the God Man. This followed the
prophecy of Amos: "On that day, says the Lord God, I will make the
sun set at midday and cover the earth with darkness in broad day-
light" (Amos 8:9; cf. Joel 2:10; 3:15; Isa. 13:10).
 A great length of time seems to have passed between the third
and fourth words spoken by Christ from the cross. As the end of his
life drew near, Christ's sufferings intensified and he observed a long
silence. Some of the crowd around the cross grew tired and left.
The Roman soldiers became bored, but the enemies of Christ were
determined to see him dead. Now Christ speaks mysterious words:
"My God, My God, why have you forsaken me?" (Matt. 27:46). In
death as in life Christ gave men an example of confidence in God.

I Christ is a model of confidence in God.
 A. The union of Christ with his heavenly Father could not be destroyed.

1. Christ is the Son of God.
   a. All through his life Our Lord enjoyed the vision of his
      heavenly Father.
      1.) There never could be a moment when Christ did not
         possess this vision.
      2.) It would be a denial of the mystery of the Incarnation
         to say that Christ, even for a moment, lost the Beautific
         Vision.
   b. Dying on the cross, Christ was the Son of God; his Sonship
      can never be destroyed.
2. Christ spoke frequently of his union with the Father.
   a. Christ said he knew the Father.
      1.) ". . . I have a testimony greater than John's, namely, the
         works the Father has given me to accomplish" (John
         5:36).
      2.) "I say only what the Father has taught me" (John 8:28).
   b. Christ identified himself with the Father.
      1.) ". . . I came forth from God . . ." (John 8:42).
      2.) "The Father and I are one" (John 10:30).
B. Christ, dying on the cross, was confident.
   1. Christ, dying on the cross, uttered a psalm of confidence.
      a. Psalm 22 begins with the words Christ now spoke: "My
         God, my God, why have you forsaken me?" (cf. Ps. 22:1;
         Matt. 27:46).
         1.) These words from Psalm 22 describe the grief and suf-
            fering of the Messiah.
         2.) They were the first words spoken by Christ in a voice
            loud enough to be heard by many near the cross.
      b. The second part of Psalm 22 is a prayer of confidence.
         1.) In this section of Psalm 22 the Messiah is seen as victo-
            rious over his enemies.
         2.) Some of the Fathers of the Church think that Christ
            prayed this psalm in its entirety and in a voice so low
            that it was heard only by those close to his cross, i.e.
            Mary and John.
   2. Dying, Christ had complete confidence in his heavenly Fa-
      ther.
      a. Christ did not dwell on himself or his condition.
         1.) He said nothing about his rejection by his people, or
            about his condemnation by the elders, or about his be-
            ing handed over to the Gentiles.

      2.) Christ did not complain about his friends who had deserted him.

      3.) He did not express any self-pity as he died in public shame on a cross, mocked by a crowd of people.

    b. Christ died a confident person.

      1.) The fact that he remained on the cross, fulfilling the Will of the Father, proved he was not a coward or a hopeless, pathetic individual.

        (a.) His condition should arouse sorrow and pity in us.

        (b.) His condition should never lead us to deny or question his heroism.

      2.) The subsequent words of Christ show his confidence in God the Father.

II We can imitate the confidence of Christ.

  A. We face many difficulties.

    1. These difficulties are associated with every life.

      a. One difficulty is associated with the selection of a vocation to the religious life, to the married state, or to the single state.

        1.) One must determine to what state God is calling him.

        2.) To make the right choice one must know one's strengths and weaknesses.

      b. After one has chosen a vocation there are still many decisions to be made.

        1.) These arise from the nature of the life one has selected.

        2.) One must always decide how to make the best contribution to the well-being of others.

    2. Other difficulties arise from temptations to self-pity.

      a. One must realize that life will not always flow as one wishes.

        1.) Without this realization one could refuse to work or to cooperate with others.

        2.) Without this realization one may miss many opportunities for good works.

      b. It is easy to feel sorry for oneself.

        1.) Pride is injured by events or by one's friends.

        2.) Some people may never be offered a word of consolation or encouragement.

  B. We must think of Christ dying on the cross.

    1. No anaesthetic was administered to him.

a. Christ felt pain in every member of his sacred body.
b. He had no relief from pain.

2. We follow the example of Christ.

a. We unite our suffering to the pain of Christ for the glory of God.
b. No matter what difficulties we face we take up our cross and follow Christ.

1.) Christ will lead us with himself to Calvary.
2.) Christ will also lead us with himself to the resurrection.

Conclusion: Every day we can ask God, as Christ did, why we are forsaken. But this is not a cry of despair. It is a sign of courage.

THE FIFTH WORD

Introduction: It seems that the rest of the dying words of Christ were spoken in quick succession. The strength of Christ was almost exhausted, and his death was very near. "After that, Jesus, realizing that everything was now finished, said to fulfill the scripture, 'I am thirsty' " (John 19:28).

I There were both physical and moral reasons for the thirst of Christ.

A. The physical reason for the thirst of Christ was foretold by one of the prophets.

1. In his suffering Christ recalled the prophecy of his thirst.

a. The physical thirst of Christ had been foretold.

1.) ". . . they put gall in my food and in my thirst they gave me vinegar to drink" (Ps. 69:22).
2.) "My throat is dried up like baked clay, my tongue cleaves to my jaws, to the dust of death you have brought me down" (Ps. 22:16).

2. We can understand that his physical sufferings caused Christ to thirst.

a. From the Gospel accounts we know that Christ had had nothing to eat or drink since the Last Supper on the night before his crucifixion.
b. In the course of his passion Christ lost blood during the agony in the Garden, the scourging at the pillar, and the crowning with thorns; when he was nailed to the cross his

precious blood flowed from his sacred wounds.
B. There was a moral reason for the thirst of Christ.
   1. Christ thirsted for our gratitude.
      a. Our debt of gratitude originates in his friendship for us.
         1.) Christ is the true friend who gratuitously gives us his
            favors.
           (a.) Christ is not concerned for himself, nor does he
              count the cost to himself as he gives us his gifts.
           (b.) There is no self-seeking or self-serving in Christ.
         2.) Christ loves us without limit; as St. John tells us: "He
            had loved his own in the world, and would show his
            love for them to the end" (John 13:1).
      b. Christ wishes to share everything he has with us.
         1.) He lived a divine life and he died on a cross that we
            may live the life of grace.
         2.) His death unified the sacraments by which we are
            born to a supernatural life and continue to live in that
            state.
         3.) Christ died in order to share his eternal happiness
            with us.
   2. On Calvary Christ's moral thirst was intense.
      a. His mother and a very few friends were with him.
      b. For the most part there was no relief for the moral thirst
         endured by Christ.
         1.) Some of the leaders of the people had succeeded in
            their efforts to arouse the crowd against Christ.
         2.) It is possible that some of the people for whom Christ
            had worked miracles also joined in the insults hurled at
            him.
         3.) The cheap wine offered to Christ (cf. Matt. 27:48) by
            one of the bystanders symbolizes the indifference and
            ingratitude Christ received.

II Our gratitude satisfies the thirst of Christ.
   A. We offer Christ our gratitude for our baptism.
      1. The Fathers of the Church saw the sacrament of baptism in
         the water that flowed from the side of Christ.
         a. In the death of Christ we receive the gift of divine life.
         b. That divine life is conferred on us in the sacrament of bap-
           tism.
      2. We offer our gratitude to Christ by our fidelity to our

baptismal promises.
   a. We continue to renounce Satan by our cooperation with the grace God gives us to conquer temptation.
   b. Our baptismal consecration to God continues by our acceptance of each inspiration of his grace.

B. We offer Christ our gratitude for the Holy Eucharist.
  1. The Fathers of the Church saw the Holy Eucharist in the precious blood flowing from the Sacred Heart of Christ.
  2. We can offer Christ the Holy Eucharist in gratitude for all his gifts.
   a. When we think of all that Christ has done for us we realize the impossibility of giving him adequate gratitude.
   b. While Christ does not demand the impossible, we can satisfy his thirst by offering any Mass we attend in a spirit of gratitude.
   c. When we recieve Holy Communion we can offer Christ our gratitude.
    1.) In our own words we can thank Christ for all his gifts.
    2.) We can offer Christ a heart willing to be grateful because the desire to thank him is itself an act of gratitude.

Conclusion: Christ dying on the cross said: "I am thirsty" (John 19:28). We do not extend to him a sponge soaked in our wine; rather, we offer him our gratitude.

THE SIXTH WORD

Introduction: The darkness deepens in the midafternoon. The death of Christ is only moments away. Our Lord lifts up his head. He sees the scene around him. He views his life. He had done all that had been asked of him. It is over; there is nothing left to be done. Christ declares: "Now it is finished" (John 19:30). He has persevered.

I Christ manifests the virtue of perseverance.
  A. The virtue of perseverance is concerned with the difficult things.
   1. To acquire virtue is difficult.
    a. An individual must control his appetite if he is to live a

virtuous life.

   b. Our associations with others must be directed by reason and justice if we are to live virtuously among people.

2. Perseverance is the virtue that helps one to tolerate the delays encountered as he attempts to acquire virtue.

   a. It takes times to acquire virtue.

      1.) When a person makes a resolution it takes time before he can carry it out.

      2.) To acquire a virtue one must repeat the action of that virtue frequently over a long period of time.

   b. A person encounters many difficulties as he strives to live a virtuous life.

      1.) One must face the failures of his efforts; such failures are caused by inexperience or human weakness.

      2.) In the practice of virtue one may encounter difficulties caused by other people.

         (a.) These do not spring from deliberate malice.

         (b.) Such difficulties exist because others do not understand our goals or because they fail to cooperate with us.

B. Christ gives us the example of perseverance.

1. Throughout his life Christ gave examples of perseverance.

   a. He did not anticipate the moment selected by the Father for the Passion.

      1.) He spoke about doing the Father's Will.

      2.) Christ waited until his hour had come before he freely laid down his life.

   b. Christ tolerated the delays caused by others.

      1.) He tolerated the insults of the Scribes and Pharisees.

      2.) He took pains to explain time and again that his kingdom was not of this world.

      3.) Christ performed miracles and took the time to explain that he was doing the works of the Father.

2. Christ gave us an example of perseverance as he died on the cross.

   a. Death by crucifixion is cruel and very slow.

      1.) Christ endured the intense agony of pain in every member of his body.

      2.) Christ suffered as he heard the insults, the mockery, the scornful remarks, and the blasphemy uttered by soldiers, priests, and people.

      b. Christ endured this agony.

        1.) He offered himself for the very people who were insulting him.

        2.) Christ did not come down off the cross; he did not interfere with the Will of the Father.

      c. Christ died with the assurance that he had done all he could. "Jesus, realizing that everything was now finished . . . Then he lowered his head and delivered over his spirit" (John 19:28,30).

II We need the virtue of perseverance.

  A. The work of our sanctification takes time.

    1. The work of our sanctification is not accomplished overnight.

      a. We need time to know ourselves and to understand our tendencies to virtue as well as our strength of will.

      b. We need time to perfect the virtues to which we are inclined by temperament, by training, and by the graces God has given us.

      c. We need time to build defenses against temptation and the inclination toward sin.

    2. We realize that it takes time to acquire and perfect all the virtues.

      a. Our sanctification does not consist in the practice of one virtue.

      b. Sanctification requires that we live according to all the virtues in all the circumstances of life.

  B. The virtue of perseverance allows us to tolerate the delays we encounter in our struggles to achieve sanctification.

    1. Among these delays are the disturbances that hinder our prayers.

      a. Some person may interrupt our prayers with a question or a desire for conversation, but we want to pray.

      b. Noises in the church during Mass may distract us.

        1.) We must struggle to control our temper on these occasions.

        2.) We must make a serious effort to concentrate on our prayers.

    2. Perhaps one of the greatest delays we encounter in striving for sanctification is "daydreaming."

       a. A "daydream" can be any fantasy in which the individual
         is the hero.
       b. It is a longing for "the things that might have been."
       c. These "daydreams" come from a refusal to face the truth
         about ourselves.
    3. Perseverance helps us to accept these interruptions along the
      way to sanctification.
       a. Perseverance allows us to see these interruptions for what
         they are.
       b. Perseverance allows us to control the interruptions and
         then start again to pray or to perform some work of char-
         ity.

Conclusion: When we have persevered in life and the moment
comes for us to die, we shall say with Christ: "It is finished" (John
19:30).

THE SEVENTH WORD

Introduction: The death of Christ is now only seconds away. St.
Matthew and St. Mark say that Christ uttered a loud cry (Matt. 27:
50; Mark 15:37) and then gave up his spirit. St. Luke tells us: "Jesus
uttered a loud cry and said 'Father, into your hands I commend
my spirit'. After he said this, he expired" (Luke 23:46). During his
life Christ taught men how to live. In his death Christ taught us how
to die.

I In his death Christ taught us how to die.
  A. Christ died with perfect resignation to the Will of his heavenly
    Father.
    1. The Father willed the death of Christ.
      a. For all eternity the Father willed the sacrifice of his Son on
        the cross.
      b. All the circumstances surrounding the death of Christ
        were willed by the Father.
        1.) Through prophecy and the signs and symbols of the
          Old Testament the Father revealed his Will for his Son.
        2.) During his life Christ called attention to the way he
          must die.
          (a.) ". . . Jesus (the Messiah) started to indicate to his

disciples that he must go to Jerusalem and suffer greatly there at the hands of the elders, the chief priests, and the scribes, and be put to death . . ." (Matt. 16:21).

(b.) "The Son of Man is going to be delivered into the hands of men who will put him to death . . ." (Matt. 17:22,23).

(c.) ". . . the Son of Man will be handed over to the chief priest and scribes, who will condemn him to death. They will turn him over to the Gentiles to be made sport of and flogged and crucified." (Matt. 20:18,19).

2. With perfect resignation to the Will of his heavenly Father, Christ accepted his death.

a. Earlier Christ had escaped from those who wished to put him to death (cf. John 10:39).

b. Christ had refused to go to Jerusalem on one occasion ". . . because the time is not yet ripe for me" (John 7:8).

c. The whole scene of the crucifixion shows the perfect resignation of Christ to the Will of the heavenly Father.

1.) Finally and deliberately Christ committed his soul to his Father's hands.

2.) With free deliberation Christ bowed his head and died.

B. Christ died with confidence in his heavenly Father.

1. Christ offered himself to the heavenly Father.

a. Christ offered himself for the glory of the heavenly Father.

1.) He made restitution to God for the sins of men.

2.) Christ satisfied the decree of the heavenly Father for the salvation of the human race.

b. Christ's sacrifice of himself is the sign of his love for his Father.

2. Christ died confident of the Father's love for him.

a. Christ placed himself in the Father's hands.

b. It was in the hands of his Father that Christ found his security.

II Christ's death is an example for us.

A. Each one of us faces knowingly that reality, death.

1. Each one of us is certain that a moment will come when he

will die.

    a. We know that no one can escape death.

    b. We are all under the law of death.

  2. No one of us knows what the circumstances of his death will be.

    a. God keeps hidden from us the details of the last moments we shall have on earth.

    b. This ignorance can be frightening.

      1.) We ask questions about death for which there are no answers, i.e., we ask how, when, and where we shall die.

      2.) We can become afraid of death.

        (a.) We ask what death will be like.

        (b.) We wonder if we shall be prepared to face God.

B. We can die with a Christlike resignation and confidence.

  1. We can die with a Christlike resignation to the Will of God.

    a. We must develop this habit now.

      1.) We can unite all our actions to the Mass that is being said somewhere in the world at the present moment.

      2.) We can unite ourselves to Christ and accept the moment of our death as it will come from the hand of God.

        (a.) We can unite the moment of our death with the Mass that will be in progress somewhere as we are dying.

        (b.) Frequently renewing this intention assures us that our intention will be effective as we lie dying.

        (c.) We know that the Mass is the same sacrifice as that of the cross.

    b. We unite ourselves with Christ in life and in death.

      1.) Our dispositions will grow to be more like his.

      2.) Our death, like our life, will be one with his death.

  2. We can die with a Christlike confidence.

    a. We can form this habit now, during our lives.

      1.) We can constantly think of the blessings that God has given us and will continue to give us.

      2.) We can come to realize that God does not abandon us.

    b. We place our security in God.

      1.) God always answers our prayers.

      2.) Living in union with Christ we are free from danger.

        (a.) The habit of uniting ourselves to Christ removes

fear from our souls.
    (b.) In union with Christ we are protected from evil.
  3.) The habit will remain with us at the moment of our death.

Conclusion: Living in union with Christ will enable us to die in union with Christ. With Christ we can say: "Father, into your hands I commend my spirit" (Luke 23:46).

HOLY SATURDAY

Introduction: The Vigil of Easter is the most solemn and impressive liturgical celebration of the year. It commemorates the most important of all the Christian mysteries, the resurrection of Christ. For, as St. Paul observes, if Christ is not risen from the dead then our faith is vain (cf. I Cor. 15:14). Moreover the celebration of baptism during the vigil liturgy enriches its content. Yet the theological substance of this observance is not speculative; rather it has a practical value in the life of one who in baptism dies and rises with Christ.

I Baptism is an incorporation into Christ.
  A. This incorporation is a spiritual rebirth.
    1. "I solemnly assure you, no one can enter into God's kingdom without being begotten of water and Spirit" (John 3:5).
      a. Our Lord insists that membership in the kingdom of God demands more than that a person be impressed by Christ's miracles.
      b. Citizenship in the kingdom of God requires a spiritual rebirth, i.e., being "begotten from above" (cf. John 1:12-13; 3:3).
    2. In the sacrament of baptism we are intimately united with Christ and with one another.
      a. "It was in one Spirit that all of us whether Jew or Greek, slave or free, were baptized into one body. All of us have been given to drink of the one Spirit" (I Cor. 12:13).
        1.) The sacrament of baptism incorporates the Christian into the risen, glorified body of Christ.
        2.) The Church is the Mystical Body of Christ because it is composed of all who share the life of the glorified Christ.

    b. "All of you who have been baptized into Christ have clothed yourselves with him" (Gal. 3:27).
       1.) One who is baptized must publicly manifest his union with Christ.
       2.) Baptized into Christ, a person must have the moral values of Christ.
B. Incorporation into Christ reproduces in the soul the death and resurrection of Christ.
    1. The baptized soul, incorporated into Christ, reproduces in his life the death of Christ.
      a. "I have been crucified with Christ" (Gal. 2:19).
      b. This is a mystical crucifixion and death for a Christian.
       1.) The baptized soul dies to selfishness and rededicates himself to the service of his neighbor.
       2.) The Christian dies to the inclination to injustice, cowardice, self-indulgence, folly, impatience, and unkindness.
    2. Incorporated into Christ, the baptized soul shares the resurrection of Christ.
      a. The spiritual life of grace, which begins with the sacrament of baptism, is perfected in eternal glory.
       1.) The glory of the risen Christ is eternal.
       2.) Baptism impresses on the soul a sacramental character which is eternal.
      b. The person who believes and is baptized will be saved (cf. Mark 16:16).
       1.) "O death, where is your victory? O death, where is your sting?" (I Cor. 15:55).
       2.) The serpent in the garden of Paradise leaves his venom —death—in the human race.
         (a.) The serpent of the garden of Paradise is conquered by the death and resurrection of Christ.
         (b.) The venom of the serpent can no longer harm those who are incorporated into Christ.

II The baptized soul lives a new life.
  A. The baptized person enters the glorified life of Christ.
    1. "He brought us to life with Christ when we were dead in sin. By this favor you were saved. Both with and in Christ Jesus he raised us up and gave us a place in the heavens" (Eph. 2:5-6).

   a. The truth that we are raised up with Christ dominates the
      life of those who are reborn in Christ.
      1.) Day by day such a soul is spiritually renewed (cf. II
          Cor. 4:16).
      2.) One is stimulated to imitate Christ in his daily actions
          (cf. Rom. 8:29; Col. 1:15; II Cor. 3:18).
      3.) The image of God is restored in the soul of one who, in-
          fluenced by the risen Christ, is incorporated into
          Christ (cf. Col. 3:10).
   b. The conviction that one who is baptized is thereby raised
      up with Christ governs the conduct of a person's life.
      1.) The heart of the baptized person is set "on what per-
          tains to higher realms where Christ is seated at God's
          right hand" (Col. 3:1).
      2.) The truth of our incorporation into the risen Christ is
          the source of our hope for glorification in heaven.
          (a.) Union with the glorified Christ is the promise of
               our glory. "God has fashioned us for this very thing
               and has given us the spirit as a pledge of it" (II Cor.
               5:5).
          (b.) The mystery which is now hidden will be revealed
               in the final resurrection: "When Christ our life ap-
               pears, then you shall appear with him in glory"
               (Col. 3:4).
2. The baptized form one body with Christ.
   a. "There is no Greek or Jew here, circumcised or uncircum-
      cised, foreigner, Scythian, slave, or freeman. Rather,
      Christ is everything in all of you" (Col. 3:11).
   b. "Through him we both have access in one Spirit to the Fa-
      ther" (Eph. 2:18).
B. The baptized person lives as a citizen of the kingdom of heav-
   en.
   1. "Let us celebrate the feast not with the old yeast, that of cor-
      ruption and wickedness, but with the unleavened bread of
      sincerity and truth" (I Cor. 5:8).
      a. "Sincerity" signifies "purity of intention," i.e., the per-
         formance by the Christian of all his works for the glory of
         God.
      b. "Truth" should be characteristic of the Christian.
         1.) "Truth" is the search for God with an undivided heart.
         2.) "Truth" also signifies fidelity to the Law of God.

        3.) "Truth" also means acting toward one's neighbor with good will and kindness.

2. As a worthy citizen of the kingdom of God, the baptized person is interested in the welfare of that kingdom.

    a. On this earth the baptized person is not exempt from suffering.

        1.) The baptized person knows that like Christ he must suffer before he enters the kingdom of heaven (cf. Luke 24:26).

        2.) The baptized soul uses his suffering for the advantage of the Church: "I fill up what is lacking in the sufferings of Christ for the sake of his body, the Church (Col. 1:24).

    b. The acts of fraternal charity performed by the baptized extend the kingdom of God on earth.

        1.) Such acts of charity imitate the good deeds of Christ which announced the presence of the kingdom of God among men.

        2.) Acts of charity bring the goodness of God and his peace into the hearts of men.

Conclusion: Tonight at this Easter Vigil we celebrate our new life of grace in the risen Christ. "We know that we have passed from death to life . . ." (I John 3:14). "Let us celebrate the feast not with the old yeast, that of corruption and wickedness, but with the unleavened bread of sincerity and truth" (I Cor. 5:8).

EASTER SUNDAY

If one wishes, the outline presented for the Easter Vigil on Holy Saturday may be used today. Since we are asked to renew our baptismal promises on Easter Sunday, the Holy Saturday outline would be appropriate for today's homily or meditation.

EASTER SUNDAY

Introduction: Easter is a feast of joy which offers us the promise of renewal. In this spirit the Easter Liturgy invites us to renew our baptismal promises. The ceremony of the Easter celebration renews the grace of our baptism. It renews our consecration to God. It renews our hope for eternal life. Easter is a feast of renewal.

I Easter is a feast of baptismal renewal.
  A. In a spirit of faith we renew our baptismal promises.
    1. The renewal of the baptismal promises is an integral part of the Easter Liturgy.
      a. When we receive baptism we may not be fully aware of the greatness of this sacrament.
        1.) Many of us received the sacrament of baptism when we were infants.
        2.) If we receive the sacrament of baptism as adults we are not always aware of its spiritual richness.
      b. Today we renew our baptismal vows.
        1.) The renewal of our baptismal vows fixes in our minds the importance of the sacrament.
        2.) We participate in today's ceremony to draw from baptism its special graces.
    2. We must make our renewal in a spirit of faith.
      a. Our faith leads us to appreciate the meaning of this ceremony and the importance of the sacrament of baptism throughout life.
      b. Faith, exercised during this ceremony, intensifies the desire of each one of us for the spiritual renewal of his life.
  B. The renewal of our baptismal vows is a rededication to the service of God.
    1. We renew the renunciation of our spiritual enemies.
      a. This renunciation is not a formula for a negative approach to life.
      b. This part of the baptismal renewal is a victory that places us once again with Christ.
        1.) This renunciation is our victory over the world; in us Christ continues to overcome the world (cf. John 16:33).
        2.) By the baptismal renewal we recall our victory with

Christ over Satan (cf. John 16:11).

3.) In this ceremony of baptismal renewal we conquer sin with Christ. "God gave you new life in company with Christ. He pardoned all our sins. He canceled the bond that stood against us with all its claims, snatching it up and nailing it to the cross" (Col. 2:13,14).

2. We dedicate ourselves to the service of God.

a. The renewal of our baptismal promises is our public admission that we belong entirely to God.

b. As the resurrection of Christ is the triumph of the heavenly power over the earthly, so baptism is the triumph of the divine over the human.

1.) In our baptismal consecration we dedicate our souls to the service of God. Living the theological virtues of faith and love, we reproduce in our lives the divine life.

2.) The faculties of the body are consecrated to the service of Christ; as St. Paul observes: "As you well know we have our citizenship in heaven. . . . Conduct yourselves, then, in a way worthy of the gospel of Christ" (Phil. 3:20; 1:27).

II Through faith, hope, and charity we live continuously in the spirit of this Easter baptismal renewal.

A. The renewal of our baptism on Easter pledges us to seek the things of heaven.

1. We remind ourselves, that human as we are, we are the children of God.

a. Christ shares our weakness that we may share his power.

1.) "It is true he was crucified out of weakness, but he lives by the power of God. We too are weak in him, but we live with him by God's power in us" (II Cor. 13:4).

(a.) Our Lord did not use his divine power before his resurrection (cf. II Cor. 8:9; Phil. 2:5-8). In his human nature Christ allowed us to see his weakness as he died on the cross.

(b.) We do penance during Lent that we may die to our human weaknesses.

2.) No human power was the cause of the resurrection of Christ (cf. Rom. 1:4; I Cor. 6:14).

b. As the children of God we live by the power of God.

   1.) We share the suffering and burial of Christ that we may die to human weakness.

   2.) By the power of God we share the resurrection of Christ to live as the children of God.

  2. Today we renew our baptism to live as the children of God.

   a. Now we seek our happiness not in earthly things, but in heaven where we shall possess God eternally.

   b. Filled with the thoughts and desires of heaven, the soul is no longer disturbed or disquieted by the thoughts of past sins.

B. Through faith, hope, and charity we live by the power God gives his children.

  1. Through the risen Christ, God gives us power to live a supernatural life.

   a. "Be steadfast and persevering, my beloved brothers, fully engaged in the works of the Lord. You know that your toil is not in vain when it is done in the Lord" (I Cor. 15:58).

   b. The Christian life is a difficult one, but lived in Christ it is not impossible.

    1.) Faith in the power of Christ enables the soul to be steadfast and persevering.

    2.) Charity prompts the soul to abound in the works of the Lord.

    3.) Hope gives the assurance that one's life and labor are not in vain.

  2. Living with the power that God gives his children changes our view of life.

   a. Through the virtue of faith the Christian knows he shares the life of the risen Christ.

    1.) The Christian views all the experiences of his life as steps toward that final moment when Christ will come again.

    2.) Christ is the first fruit of the resurrection; in him and through him all Christians are dedicated to God. Through Christ the Christian rises in glory (cf. I Cor. 15:14,20).

   b. The virtue of hope is a characteristic of a Christian exile on earth: "He (Christ) will give a new form to this lowly body of ours and remake it according to the pattern of his glorified body, by his power to subject everything to himself" (Phil. 3:21).

c. The Christian dedicates himself to renew his outlook on life by love.

1.) "Put to death whatever in your nature is rooted in earth . . ." (Col. 3:5).

2.) The resurrection of Christ and our baptismal renewal bring us to a new life of love: "Because you are God's chosen ones, holy and beloved, clothe yourselves with heartfelt mercy, with kindness, humility, meekness, and patience. Bear with one another; forgive whatever grievances you have against one another (Col. 3:12-13).

Conclusion: On this day of renewal we rededicate ourselves to God and to the Christian life. We know that "we have our citizenship in heaven. . . . Conduct yourselves, then, in a way worthy of the gospel of Christ" (Phil. 1:27).

EASTER SUNDAY

Introduction: On this feast of Easter we celebrate the resurrection of Christ to a new life. We also celebrate our baptism by the renewal of our baptismal vows. We celebrate our new life of grace. This renewal of the promises we made in baptism is the rededication of ourselves to live perfectly the life of grace.

Grace is our paschal life by which we live the death and resurrection of Christ. The renewal of our baptismal vows is a promise that we shall live in Christ, and it expresses our desire to persevere in this life.

I In the sacrament of baptism we share the grace of the resurrection.

A. The sacrament of baptism associates us with the life of the resurrection.

1. The sacrament of baptism introduces us to the resurrection of Christ.

a. "Through baptism into his death we were buried with him, so that just as Christ was raised from the dead by the glory of the Father, we too might live a new life" (Rom. 6:4).

1.) The water of the sacrament of baptism cleanses the soul of the dead work of sin.

    2.) The soul leaves the baptismal font in the new life of
     grace.
   b. The sacrament of baptism exposes us to the obligations of
    the supernatural life of grace.
    1.) In receiving the sacrament of baptism we are clothed
     with a white robe and we are asked to hold a lighted
     candle.
    2.) The white robe is a symbol of the baptized soul's inno-
     cence which he must preserve; the light of the candle
     represents the grace of God in the baptized soul which
     he must not extinguish.
  2. In the sacrament of baptism the soul first experiences the
   power of God.
   a. "Just as Christ was raised from the dead by the glory of
    the Father, we too might live a new life" (Rom. 6:4).
    1.) St. Paul in this verse attributes the resurrection to the
     power of the Father.
    2.) St. Paul follows the custom of the Old Testament
     which ascribes its great miracles to the Father.
   b. The glory of the Father shines in the risen Christ (cf. II
    Cor. 4:6).
    1.) This power of the risen Christ is the ability to com-
     municate life to others (cf. Rom. 1:4; I Cor. 15:45).
    2.) The divine life is given to the baptized soul who is glo-
     rified with Christ (cf. II Cor. 3:18; Rom. 8:17).
    3.) Just as the power of the Father is the cause of the resur-
     rection of Christ, so the power of the Father raises the
     baptized soul from sin.
B. The sacrament of baptism opens the soul to the influence of
 God.
  1. The sacrament of baptism purifies and sanctifies the soul
   who receives it.
   a. The sacrament of baptism purifies the soul.
    1.) The sacrament of baptism washes the soul from sin in
     the name of Christ.
    2.) The sacrament of baptism is the birth of the soul in
     water and the Spirit (cf. John 3:5).
   b. The sacrament of baptism sanctifies the soul.
    1.) The grace of the sacrament of baptism makes the soul
     an adopted child of God (cf. I John 3:1).
    2.) "In the sacrament of baptism the Holy Spirit impresses

a seal on the soul" (cf. Eph. 1:13; 4:30; II Cor. 1:22).

3.) The grace of the sacrament of baptism is the passage from the darkness of sin to the light of the risen Christ (cf. Eph. 5:8-14).

2. The grace of baptism consecrates the soul to God.

a. The baptized soul is united with Christ.

b. The soul is subjected to the influence of the Three Divine Persons.

1.) The baptized soul, because it is a child of God, is directed by the Father.

2.) As co-heir with the Son the baptized shares the passion, death, and resurrection of Christ.

3.) Filled with the Holy Spirit, the Christian experiences the divine life as far as this is humanly possible.

II The grace of the resurrection develops day by day in the soul of the baptized.

A. The baptized soul lives according to the Spirit.

1. "Those who live according to the flesh are intent on the things of the flesh, those who live according to the spirit, on those of the spirit. The tendency of the flesh is toward death but that of the spirit toward life and peace" (Rom. 8:5-6).

a. The Spirit of God is the principle of life in the soul of the baptized.

b. It is the Spirit that leads the soul to reconciliation and peace with God.

2. The influence of the Spirit in the soul does not operate automatically as a result of the sacrament of baptism.

a. The reign of the Spirit in the soul of the baptized is disputed by the influence of the flesh.

1.) "Flesh" is to be understood as self-centeredness and the evils flowing from it, which exclude the soul from the kingdom of God (cf. Gal. 5:19-21).

2.) "Those who live according to the flesh are intent on the things of the flesh. . . . The tendency of the flesh is toward death. . . . The flesh in its tendency is at enmity with God. . . those who are in the flesh cannot please God" (Rom. 8:5-8).

b. The Spirit in the soul of the baptized enables that soul to conquer the influence of the flesh and arrive at the perfection of life.

    1.) "Those who live according to the spirit (are intent) on those (things) of the spirit. . . . you are in the spirit, since the Spirit of God dwells in you. . . . If the Spirit of him who raised Jesus from the dead dwells in you, then he who raised Christ from the dead will bring your mortal bodies to life also, through his spirit dwelling in you" (Rom. 8:5-11).

    2.) "The fruit of the spirit is love, joy, generosity, faith, mildness, and chastity. . . . Those who belong to Christ Jesus have crucified their flesh with its passions and desires. Since we live by the spirit, let us follow the spirit's leads" (Gal. 5:22-25).

B. Daily the baptized soul is open to the influence of the Holy Spirit.

    1. The baptized soul disposes itself for the influence of the Holy Spirit by faith.

        a. Faith expresses a willingness of the soul to be open to the inspiration of the Holy Spirit.

        b. The soul directed by faith accepts the Word of God in its daily life.

            1.) To such a soul the words of Christ serve as the guide to conduct.

            2.) By applying the merits of Christ to its life, the baptized soul seeks to please the Father in all its activity.

    2. The Holy Spirit influences the soul that is subject to Christ.

        a. Such a soul accepts Christ completely.

        b. The entire being, mind, memory, will, and imagination are influenced by the presence of the Holy Spirit in the soul.

Conclusion: By our baptism we participate in the resurrection of Christ. The Spirit, given to the soul in baptism, leads the individual to the perfect participation in the resurrection on the last day. Since we live by the spirit, let us follow the spirit's leads" (Gal. 5:25).